WE 3

WENDELL ETERNAL

Volume I

Authored 2023

ORDER OF THE HIDDEN

"If you write about their life, they'll all hate you. If you tell them a lie, they'll all embrace you."

THE BOY AND THE PENDANT

The constant gnawing and gnashing of teeth became unbearable. The hunger headaches and stomach pains were at least livable. There was only one thing Puma was not willing to tolerate an instant longer. HIKERS, that left their trash all over his mountain. The mere fact that they encroached on his territory marked them for death. The elders told Puma not to kill man. "For man will kill many of us in return." Puma scoffed at this notion, for most of the lions were starving and dying anyway.

The time for retaliation was rapidly approaching. Puma was not the biggest Mountain Lion, but he was certainly the fastest. Humans had renamed his mountain and set up their encampments all over. Puma considered himself better than the rest of his elk, a true big cat amongst kittens. The impossible was accomplished in his eyes. Others exactly like him had not lived long. A highly melanated Mountain Lion sticks out like a sore thumb in daylight. All his life he sacrificed. Never stepping a paw in the sunlight. Never frolicking about while others courted mates. Eternals time is now, were his last thoughts before he slept.

As the wind chilled, the birds singing began to dissipate. The temperature felt exactly right as the owl hooted in the moonlight. Puma's stomach began to growl. His mouth began to salivate as he envisioned fresh flesh. His cave, although a great hiding spot, was horribly uncomfortable. Puma let out muffled roar as he began to stretch his muscles and groom himself. The fear of death had escaped him. Why should one fear the natural cycle of life? True enough, he did not want to be murdered on man's terms. Puma had no qualms with his own death as long has vengeance was fulfilled prior to his life cycle ending. The big cat flexed his claws in and out as he started his mission.

As he slipped out of his cave, he sniffed Teeka close by. Teeka was the only lioness he granted safe passage on his hold of the mountain. A beautiful lioness with white tips on all her paws. Teeka, the best hunter he had ever seen, was in heat. Teeka had been waiting for three of her cycles to bond with Puma. The possibility his cubs may come out like him made him shudder. A few nights earlier Puma had consented to her request. This action was meaningless to him for he had not enjoyed it. For there was no courtship, no catch and release, no chasing. Puma thought back to that night in his cave. He was thinking about human flesh as she purred ever so softly. Puma pushed those thoughts out of his mind as he darted towards the human encampment.

Teeka never followed Puma, for she knew his heart was as black as the coat he dawned. Her love for him was based on what he could evolve into. Not for what others knew him to be. Teeka slinked away as Puma started his stalking rituals. Puma could smell man a mile away. Such noisy wasteful creatures, Puma thought. As he approached the retched creatures the first quarter moon dimly lit their nesting areas. No matter, his vision increased with the coming of darkness. The thought of his canines sinking in flesh gave him a feeling of euphoria. As the big cat began to creep ever closer, the smell of rotting flesh and plants numbed his nose. Humans, he thought, such disgusting helpless creatures in my domain. As Puma approached the encampment the sheer size of the human's fire frightened him. This was it, could he really succeed? The humans had the fire god on their side, and she was enormous.

 I am the lord of this mountain. My hate goes beyond my fear of the fire god. I will have my vengeance no matter the consequences. Just as those thoughts raced through Puma's head, thunder cracked, and mother water began fighting the fire god. This was The Creator encouraging Puma. The probability of humans tracking him in this weather was extremely low indeed. Finally, the gods had granted Puma his perfect time to strike. As the thunder began cracking with the lightning strikes, a woman emerged from her nesting area. Puma concentrated all his efforts into coiling his muscles for a spring attack. The woman began to mutter things incoherently as she threw more plants into the giant fire. An instant Moor and the back of her neck would be in his jowls.

 The woman disappeared, only smoke was where she once was. Puma was in shock. He never saw a human move so fast. Where did she go? What was happening? In an instant the woman reappeared holding a man child in her arms. The man child was trembling as the woman began to chant louder and louder. Puma could hardly contain himself. Two kills for the price of one. The woman pulled out shiny metal and sunk it deep into the man child, killing him instantly. The woman placed the child in the cauldron halfway submerged. Puma took a step back as his cat stinks warned him. He no longer wanted the woman. The child was dead, thus could not scream out. The woman disappeared again as Puma leapt upon the slain man child. Puma let out a low growl as his paws seared from the hot metal. Just as Puma darted off with his prize, the woman reappeared screaming something at him. "I CURSE YOU WITH THE SACRIFICE HALF MOON BLOOD!"

THE BOY AND THE PENDANT TOO

One month had passed since Puma had completed his mission. He was so proud of himself and delighted that no one knew his secret. Puma had taken the man child and devoured him. When the flesh was gone, he crushed the bones to lap up the marrow. There was nothing left of the man child but the powder of his bones. The powder of the man child's bones enticed him so much, that he often rolled around in them. The human woman had brought no hunters, no trappers, this puzzled Puma. Oh well, a gain gotten in secret is better than a loss in public, as he thought to himself. Maca Ina had granted him safe passage. All was right in Puma's realm. Teeka's stomach had begun to swell with his cubs. Puma began to crave the sunlight more and more each day. This worried Teeka immensely. There were no worries in Puma's mind, if he died now, he would be a happy big cat.

As the first quarter moon began to emerge, Puma was not feeling TOO well. He sniffed the air. Could it be? HUNTERS! Close, so remarkably close. Puma had only been this close to humans once in his life. The night he had taken the boy. The mind of Puma raced frantically. Man was in his cave, and they could have their fire sticks pointed at him. Puma calmed himself and remembered the cycle of life. He had made his choice. The only thoughts in his mind were to warn Teeka before his demise. Puma thought to himself, "I will let out a loud roar and face the fire sticks. I will kill at least one of the intruders." Just as Puma let out a loud roar, a child's voice could be heard saying, "FLEE TEEKA!" How could this child make his noise known to my ears? Why had the fire sticks not bitten him?

The air was stale and brisk as it blew through Pumas' cave. What was going on? Puma had a new feeling; he was vibrating uncontrollably. The big cats' thoughts were scattered. Puma constantly searched through his life cycle encounters. He wanted to know what this horrible feeling was. Finally, he remembered! Many moons ago Puma had fallen into Godmother water. He was just a cub then. Puma had fallen into the water, just as the leaves were falling off the spirit trees. His mother, Sheeba, had pulled him out of the water just in time. That was many moons ago, Puma thought to himself. Why now do I have this sensation through my bones as if my fur has been ripped from me? Puma licked his paw and immediately let out a yelp! They have got me, the humans are so close I licked their flesh. ROAR! Teeka had returned and she seemed pissed. Why had she not heeded my warning? Can she not smell the humans are upon me?

  Something strange was going on. This was a feeling he had experienced before. This was FEAR. Terror was in Pumas' chest. Teeka silently traversed their cave. The wind howled as the fresh air engulfed Pumas nose. Teeka was on the prowl; she would risk her life and that of their seeds to save him. Puma felt weak from the confusion in his mind, nevertheless he was ready to spring. Teeka could smell the humans in her den. This was her lair, she would rip the humans apart, or die trying. This is the natural cycle of life. The Elders had guided her well. "Eat or be eaten. Take not waste not." The smell of the humans was strong indeed. They were in her lair, and they had no fire sticks. Teeka thought to herself, "Puma will be so proud of me."

  Puma let out a low growl, as the man child spoke again. He heard that same noise he unbelievably could inner stand. "Teeka is that you?" Teeka froze in her tracks. This was not humans. This was a man child and he seemed frightened. The lioness glided silently to the man child. Teeka lay less than one cats length from the man child. Her tail flopped side to side in a relaxed manner as she observed this oddity. The man child had no fur and no coverings, only the shiny metal upon his chest. One third of Teeka's gestation period had passed. She could now sense the cubs inside her. Teeka held no hate in her heart towards the children of men. Only curiosity and fascination were her thoughts. She let out a low purr to alert the man child of her presence. Puma heard Teeka's growl and the uncontrollable vibrating returned. The vibration Teeka emitted hit Puma in his gut as he began to urinate. This humming tone he clearly remembered from times past. This was the sound Teeka let out when she was playing with her food!

The big cat took his paw and inserted it in his mouth. There was that familiar taste again. "It" is not human. The taste was that of the man child he had eaten just a half-moon ago. Now the gravity of his present predicament had come full circle. Puma was the prey and Teeka his adversary.

Teeka let out a loud ROAR! The man child had marked her den with his scent. All the curiosity and fascination evaporated from her mind. Her primal urge took over and it was time to feed. Puma would be so proud of her for defending their lair. The lioness leapt upon the man child. Teeka toppled him instantly. The man child screamed as Teeka pressed her paw into his chest and extended her claws. Frantically the man child's hands swiped at Teeka's whiskers. Teeka simply responded by biting off his right thumb. The taste of the man child was strangely familiar. Teeka looked into the eyes of her prey. Those eyes, she recognized those eyes. The lioness leaned in closer to smell the man child. That smell, she recognized that smell ever so faintly. The big cat retracted her claws. Suddenly Teeka felt a ping in her heart. Everything grew dark as she heard the loud crack of thunder.

Puma laid motionless as Teeka's immense weight began to smother him. The cycle of life was now complete. The hunters had exacted their revenge. Puma inner stood the noise the humans were making. They were celebrating. The loud laughter filled Pumas ears while the hunters approached their kill. The men began to flash their fire all about the cave. One of the hunters said, "Be careful. That black one is still in here. I never saw him leave."

THE BOY AND THE PENDANT STILL

_Hunter 1, we will call him Phris, neared the big cat. Phris approached Teeka with a feeling of dread and terror in his heart. Hunter 2, we will call him Tody, yelled out to Phris….” Load and lock lil bro, load, and lock.” The cave was dark and tight. Phris's knees began to buckle as his heart almost beat right out of his chest. Tody sensed his little brother's trepidation and decided to crack a joke. He said, “Wasn't that a funny thing grandma BoeDoe did to her son in law?” Phris did not want any part of the 5-year-old joke. Phris's hands began to shake and sweat profusely. This was “it”, the high of highs, the rush of rushes. Facing a black cat in a dark cave. There was only one problem, Phris was a coward, and too scared to speak the Truth. Fear had totally consumed him as he approached Teeka's carcass.

   Both hunters were cautious as they prepared for the black cat to spring from the shadows. “Cover me, Tody. I will make sure the cat is dead.” Tody steadied his rifle and prepared for the worst. Phris used his rifle to roll the big cat over. What they saw astonished them, both men let out a yelp and jumped back. Under the big cat was The Boy and the Pendant. Such a beautiful pendant reflecting off the flashlights. The hunters looked at each other with bewildered faces. Puma lied still unable to move. Puma's mind was working but his body was in shock. Figuring out that he had shapeshifted into the boy he had eaten, left him paralyzed. “What Tody? Do you think he is alive?” Tody, the resident addict, was more worried about the pendant upon the boy's neck. “One way to find out lil bro. Take that pendant off his neck first. I will cover you.”

   Phris reached for the pendant. Soon as his hand made contacted the pendant…. ROAR!!!!! In an instant, Phris was now in the woods of Columbo County. Another loud roar ripped through Phris's mind, as he hopped through the woods. Phris was a rabbit now and Puma, the black cat was hunting him. Puma leapt upon the rabbit, killing him instantly with a bite to the neck. Phris released the pendant. He clutched at his heart as his hair turned white. His last words were, "It is him. IT'S HIM!" Tody was now mesmerized, in a trance like state. Three life forms lay motionless before him as he eased backwards out of the cave.

Tody stood outside of the cave typing in the numbers to the park ranger. He punched the sixth number in his phone and then pressed end. Addiction would not let Tody follow the proper procedures. He did love his brother, but he loved to get high even more. Tody thought to himself, "I will take the boy home. I will figure out how to get the pendant off him later. Then I will come back for Phris."

Tody placed the boy on his sofa. The boy was alive although speechless. Tody lived in the middle of nowhere. Miles from the nearest road. His plan was simple. He would tie the boy up and return later to remove the pendant. While searching for rope to tie the boy up, a brilliant plan jumped in Today's mind. He would order the boy to take off the pendant. Once the boy took off the pendant, Tody would dispose of him. Phris would have to wait. Tody needed that pendant off the boy. He picked up his rifle and pointed it at Puma. "Remove the chain from your neck boy, or I'll shoot you right in the face!"

The blank stare was gone from Puma's face. With the fire stick pointed at him, he knew what the hunter wanted. Puma had no choice. He placed both his hands on the pendant and began to pull it over his head. Tody set the rifle down as he approached the boy. As soon as the pendant cleared Puma's head....... ROAR!!!!! Puma had shapeshifted back to the black cat. The pendant fell to the floor. Tody's eyes darted to the rifle. Puma was free and he knew ET! Tody reached for the rifle. Puma gave him a powerful swipe across his face. Puma's mighty paw knocked Tody's right eye clean out the socket. Puma sprung on Tody's throat and ripped most of it out with one bite. Tody lied there dying. He now knew what Phris had meant when he said, "Its Him!" The boy and the pendant were the black cat.

THIRTEEN SECONDS LATER

Puma had blacked out. He was now the boy again. Every muscle in his body contracted and burned. He let out a moan as the pain forced tears from his eyes. The big cat turned boy, was in so much pain, he could do nothing but blink his eyes. The morning turned to night as Puma remained unmoved. Shapeshifting is a power task, Puma thought to himself. A task one must not take on recklessly. Night turned to morning and Puma was abruptly awoken. BANG, BANG BANG! "Tody are you in there?" The park ranger and town sheriff were outside the door. Phris had been reported missing when he did not return from his hunting trip. The sheriff continued to beat the door vigorously. The park ranger peaked through the cabin window. "Sheriff, we have got a body. Tody's throat is ripped out and there is blood everywhere."

Both men unholstered their weapons. The sheriff kicked the door in. The park ranger shot through the opening ready to fire at anything moving. Out the corner of his eye he saw a boy push himself upright. The park ranger holstered his weapon and motioned the sheriff to come in. Two hunters in front of him and one fire stick pointed directly at him.... Puma knew it was time for the black cat to make an appearance. Just as Puma was discarding the pendant, the sheriff was holstering his weapon. ROAR!!! Puma sprinted past the two men into the Columbo woods.

THIRTEEN SECONDS LATER AGAIN

Puma shot through the forest with one thought on his mind. TEEKA! Maybe she was just wounded, he had to get back to the lair. Puma blacked out again. This time the pain from the transformation had increased. The agony left him only one thought, "Surely I will die." The park ranger had a special number to dial if he ever saw anything unbelievable. He scoffed at the notion he would ever need such a number. Not only had he needed that number, but he had also used it as well.

Special Agent M. Swim entered Puma's glass enclosure. A boy aged no more than 13 sat before her. Puma's hands were chained to the steal table, far from his pendant. His jet-black hair and feral eyes were truly a remarkable sight. Agent Swim took her seat and removed a folder from her briefcase. "My name is Agent Swim. May I ask you your name?" Puma tried to roar but only the word Puma sprang out. "Puma huh…. what a righteously accurate name for such a talented young boy." Puma growled, "What do you want?!" "I want you Puma and I shall have you." Agent Swim pushed the folder over to Puma and asked him one question. "Would you rather rip out the throats of bad men or spend the rest of your life in this glass box?"

Puma whispered something inaudible. Agent Swim leaned in closer to the boy. She noticed he was missing his right thumb. Puma whispered again but this time Agent Swim heard two of the words. "Have You." Agent Swim was twelve inches away from Puma's face as he whispered again. This time she heard the full sentence. "I SHALL HAVE YOU!" Puma lunged at her trying to bite her mouth off. His forehead smashed against her nose as he narrowly missed biting her. Agent Swim's nose was broken, and she was knocked to the floor. Puma was hysterically trying to get his hands free so he could devour the woman. Agent Swim's eyes began to blacken as the blood flowed freely from her nose. She sat up, pulled herself into the chair and began to laugh uncontrollably with pain shed tears rolling down her rose red cheeks.

Puma calmed and looked at the human woman quizzically. "Such a delightful young man. Puma, we are going to make beautiful music together. Hunting is an art form. I will help you exact your revenge on hunters and all things outside of nature." Puma looked at the woman with a blank stare, "What's music?"

Agent Swim got up and exited the glass box. She then gave explicit instructions on how she wanted Puma to be managed over the next year. "I want an inescapable warehouse built. Populate this warehouse with the plants, trees, and game from its natural habitat. He is to be watched closely. Anytime Puma is on the hunt I want classical music to be played. The music will stop once the kill is made. Release a lioness in his enclosure so that he may sire cubs. Place a monitor in his enclosure. In the morning, this monitor will play only educational programs. At night, every night, I want some version of the Halloween movies playing." Agent Swim's superiors got wind of what she was doing. The board was called and not only her job, but her life was on the line. In Agent Swim's profession, there was no retirement plan. She knew too much. She would either be allowed to continue her work, or she would be put down.

The twelve board members took their seats. Agent M. Swim marched into the boardroom in full military garb. She had seen action in Afghanistan, if she were going to go down, it would be in full colonel dress. As she took her seat, no one spoke. In these types of meetings only the interviewee spoke. The projector was turned on. Thirteen heads turned to look at the screen. A paper was placed on the projector. The words read, "What are you doing with the boy and the pendant?" A year had passed since she first started project Puma. Countless millions had been spent and lives had been lost. During this process Agent Swim was able to accomplish her goal. She had successfully gotten Puma to accept her as his Elder.

The time was now. She would make her move. She would give the board their coveted answer. "The boy and I will make beautiful music together." Agent Swim stood up, saluted, and exited the board room. Her nerves of steel were the only things holding her together. If she was allowed to enter the elevator and return down to her office, she had passed the inquisition. Agent Swim pushed the elevator button. Her nerves beginning to unravel knowing full well a bullet could burst her skull any moment. The elevator buzzed open. She entered the elevator as the door closed behind her. Agent Swim had indeed passed her test. Instead of going to her office, she buzzed down to Puma's level. As she entered the underground square mile of forest, she called out. "Puma, Mozart is calling." A loud roar ripped through her bones. Puma sprung out of the tree above her with the pendant in his mouth. Puma had not only harnessed his powers but mastered shapeshifting as well. Puma and Agent Swim had figured out his dilemma. If the pendant remained in his mouth or upon his neck, he could stay in black cat form for hours with no ill after affects. Puma shapeshifted into the boy. He gave Agent Swim a big embrace. Then the two of them exited the facility.

MERMAID MEATS, OCEAN WATER

How do you describe a Mermaid that walks on land? To put it plainly… a fish out of water. Mermaid stumbled through life as if she were walking on sand. Where others walked easily, it was a real chore for her to keep her footing. Mermaid, such a beautiful soul, with cedar for eyes. The color of her skin was the reflection of the sun itself. The voice of an angel with a heart of gold, Mermaid, such a beautiful soul. Intellectually she was average at best. This lack of intellect stemmed mostly from a lack of interest. Mermaid would rather talk to animals instead of people. The one person she wanted to converse with was her mother. Mermaid could not understand why her mother was so concerned with the lives of other people. The weight of the mother-daughter broken bond, pulled at her heart continuously. Mermaid thought to herself, "At least I have mother nature and she will never let me down."

There is a certain kind of peace that comes with spending most of your time alone or with animals. Mermaid had this peace. Sure, her mother was never home but she did have everything she needed. The house was big, the grass was green and the shelves and cupboards full of fruits and veggies. Mermaid loved her mother so much, she pretended to understand the whole single parent thing. When in all actuality, she did not. She had told her mother before. "Mom, just get a smaller house. We can share a room and you can be home more." Instead, her mother moved them into a five-bedroom castle of a house. Mermaids house looked like it could repel a small army. Bullet proof glass and steel doors covered the openings of her home. Corporation grade lights and cameras were installed on all fronts. When Mermaid asked her mother, "Mom, why do we need all of this stuff?" Her mother had smiled at her and said, "We do not. They are just nice to have in case we ever do." This answer, like most of the answers her mother gave her, only confused her more.

Mermaid was well loved in early grade school before the other children could understand she was different. Not only did everyone always stare at her because of her looks, she also held full blown conversations with animals too. When she started high school, the bullying followed soon after. Boys were something that she liked but not as much as nature and animals. In middle school the other children just laughed and pointed at her when she talked to the animals. Everything changed when she got to high school. One single question had doomed her for perpetuity for the total of her high school days. Mermaid was once asked, "Hey Mermaid, when you talk to the animals, do they talk back?" Mermaid had replied, "Well of course silly, why else would I be talking to them?" That one answer had doomed her. Now she was the laughing stalk of the school. Sometimes kids from other schools came just to pick on her too. Mermaid knew if she stopped talking to the animals the kids would stop picking on her. The thought of that made her cry as she entered her fortress looking house.

Same routine as usual. Push play on the supercomputer refrigerator and watch the screen. Mermaid listened to her mother's message, "Hey my little swimmer, how are you? I have good news and shocking news." Mermaid pressed stop. Mermaid hated hearing her "Mothers bad news" on an empty stomach. While preparing her food, Mermaid spoke aloud to herself, "Come on mom with the unwelcome news shit. This has been going on for months on end." Once she began eating, she pressed resume and the screen clicked on. "The good news is… I am back in town. The sad news is, I am working late. I know I have been gone for a week, but I will try and make it home before you go to sleep." This infuriated Mermaid because it was an outright lie. Her mother never made it home before she fell asleep.

Mermaid finished her meal and started the long trek to her mailbox. Soon as she opens it up AGHHH!!! A rat squeaked and jumped out, nearly knocking the poor girl down. "Damn kids!" She muttered and then started to laugh. "Well, that was a good one." The rat had returned now and apologized. Then asked for some food. Mermaid replied, "Next time just lead with that. Your apology does not mean as much now." The rat replied, "Come on M. How could I know that was you? I thought that was them returning and I wanted to give them a proper scare. I really am sorry." Mermaid

gave him a piece of cheese and they said their goodbyes. The rat
went on his merry way. Jus as Mermaid was about to go back into
her fortress, she noticed she was being recorded. Her neighbor had
his phone pointed straight at her and was laughing so hard he fell.
Mermaid thought to herself, "Great! Just what I needed. I am going
viral again, for the wrong reason, AGAIN."

MERMAID MEATS, OCEAN WATER II

_When Mermaid got to school the laughing started immediately. It
got louder and louder as she approached her locker. Everyone was
watching as she noticed her lock had been removed. Mermaid
snatched open her locker and cheese fell out. She stood peering
into her locker and wondering, "How the heck did they get all that
cheese in there?" She clapped her hands and took a bow as she
proceeded to the guidance counselor's office to report the incident.
Mermaids' guidance counselor was worried about her. He told her
she displayed symptoms of disassociation. Mermaid had gotten up
and walked out while he was trying to explain disassociation to her,
as if she actually cared. Today she would not go straight home.
Mermaid wanted to walk on the beach to clear her mind.

 The sun shined brilliantly on her skin while the fresh salty air
calmed her nerves. Her inner peace returned to her as the
throbbing in her head began to dissipate. The birds hovered above
her singing their little hearts out. They were happy to see her.
Mermaid had not been to the beach in a year. Then it happened.
She heard a wave at first. Then the Ocean herself began to speak to
her. "Why are you so sad Mermaid? It is a beautiful day." Mermaid
stopped in her tracks. She looked at the ocean and the voice spoke
again. "Yes, it was me. I am Ocean, mother of all water." Mermaid
thought to herself, "Great, just what I needed. Now people are

going to see me talking to the ocean and think I am talking to myself." The voice repeated, "I know you can hear me Mermaid." Mermaid finally replied, "Nice meeting you Mother Ocean but I've got to go. I am late for my friend's party." But wait, the voice said. "I know a secret."

Mermaid sat down and said, "Go ahead. You are the ocean, so I know this is going to be good. But first tell me, how do you know my name? And do you know everyone's name?" The voice replied, "All who come to my shores or traverse upon me are known to me." "Ok, Mother Ocean, what's the secret?" "I know secrets about your mother and her mother before her." Mermaid did not like this one bit. Her mother was a very touchy subject. But she played along anyway. "Go ahead, I'm listening." The voice spoke, "Your name is Mermaid, your mother's name is Mermaid, and your grandmothers name was Mermaid as well." Mermaid stood up and said, 'Ok, I'm out. That little tidbit of info is not worth me getting picked on at school." "What is picked on at school?" Never mind Mother Ocean, I am going to be late." "Ok, my lovely darling. Before you go, I will tell you one more thing. You are a real Mermaid. Your true home is with me. This is why you are so unhappy with the land man." Mermaid headed home with thoughts in her head running wild and rough like a stormy sea. "Could it be? Am I a mermaid?"

Saturdays were her favorite days. Mermaid was ecstatic to be captain of the swim team. Sure, the other girls picked on her, but they respected the hell out of her talent. For once, the talk she had with her guidance counselor turned out to be especially useful. Mr. Elkfeather told her about the other girls from her team. They were just picking on her because it was the cool thing to do. Mermaid did not believe him at first. Then she realized something. Her teammates never picked on her at practice. This was because practice was closed. You had to be a parent or on the swim team to attend. Practice became Mermaids sanctuary once she came to this realization.

So many thoughts raced through Mermaids head as she made the mile long trek to practice. "My fingers do have extra webbing. Coach Jet had even told me so. And why were there so many mermaid named women in her family? Like, guy's name their children after themselves, right? Chicks rarely do that." The thoughts racing through her head were more like questions with no answers. Mermaid needed to focus. This was time for her to evaluate all the hard work she had been putting in. Mermaid practiced in a 50-meter pool. The best she had ever done was 149 laps. This was almost five miles. Today she would try 160 laps. The 5k mark was something she felt she had to do. Thinking about what Mother Ocean told her, had Mermaid believing that she could breathe water.

MERMAID MEATS, OCEAN GODDESS

The ocean beckoned to Mermaid like heat beckons to the sun. Three weeks had passed since she visited Ocean, Mother of All water. Wanting to know if she was really a mermaid, tugged at her heart like an ice pick. The thought of holding another conversation with Mother of all water frightened her. What if she was a mermaid? Would not kids make fun of her even more? Mermaid asked her mother about her name, their name. To which her mother replied, "A name is just a name. People make their name based on their own lives. Unless you are filthy rich your name does not mean much." This sparked a huge argument between mother and daughter. Mermaid wanted to know who could afford this castle/dungeon they were living in. If they were not filthy rich, why had her mother moved them into this expensive house? Why won't she tell me the truth about our name? Mermaid decided to go to the beach to get the answers she needed.

The ocean waves seemed to calm as soon as mermaids' feet hit the sand. The ocean looked like a calm lake on a Saturday morning. Everything was calm except for her. Mermaids heart beat out of her chest. Her hands trembled at the thought of hearing the voice. She knew once she approached, Mother of All water would be waiting. Trepidation butterflies flew up and down her spine as she approached the water's edge. The water, barely moving, calmly spoke; "Mermaid, why do you run from your true home?" The water was so calm and inviting. Mermaid had never seen the ocean this calm. The ocean had spoken but Mermaid was in a trance from the stillness of the water. "Mermaid, I can show you your true form if you just trust me." The birds chirped hysterically but Mermaid did not pay them any attention. She was ready for the big reveal.

"Ok Mother Ocean, I am ready for your wisdom. Tell me, what must I do to obtain my true form. Ocean replied, "Just come to me Mermaid. Once you are in my presence, I can show you my true form. Just follow my voice." Mermaid contemplated this as she thought about her life from being a baby all the way to this exact moment. It was so cool how all her thoughts flashed in her mind so vividly. Mermaid took off her shoes and began to glide across the water. After about a mile in her swim, Ocean Mother of All water spoke, "That's it Mermaid, you are getting closer to your truth. This time the voice scared Mermaid. The voice was stronger, and the water rippled as she heard her. Mermaid knew how far she was from the shore. Her lungs had begun to burn just as they had done when she swam five miles in the practice facility. The voice spoke again.

"Mermaid, you are indeed a true little swimmer. Your truth I shall reveal unto you now." This time the voice petrified Mermaid. The water did not ripple with the voice this time. This time the water raged, and the sun was blocked by dark clouds. Mermaid was exhausted. Her head dipped under the water. She swallowed a mouth full of water before calling out. "Mother Ocean help me please. I am drowning and I am scared!" "I am no Mother Ocean foolish child. I am Ocean, mother of all water." Just as Mermaid heard the voice, she could hear the birds chirping again. Time had slowed all the way down. Mermaid could clearly hear what the birds had been chirping about so hysterically. "It is a trick!!! Fly, fly, fly away Mermaid!" In her rush to get answers she had ignored her one faithful friend. The animals of Maca Inna.

 "I am Ocean, mother of all water. I find you guilty of the sins of your mother's mother. You are no mermaid foolish girl. YOU ARE MEATS! You are substance for my children who dwell upon my sea floor. This is your truth foolish girl. Your mother's mother betrayed the mermaids. She gave secrets to the land man. Secrets she was given out of love. This caused and effect pained my innards to know end. Your grandmother caused billions of deaths in my waters. Just as your mother caused deaths as well. Your grandmother had the gift. I called out to her once and she never stepped foot near a body of water the rest of her days. Your grandmother then passed this knowledge and name to your mother. Then your mother not believing in me, gave you the name but no KNOWLEDG!"

 Mermaids' skeleton lay still at the bottom of the ocean. Just as a crab plucked out her eye, ET happened. Lightning shot straight from the bottom of the ocean into the sky. There was no voice this time. Only words that sounded like thunder. "Ocean, Mother of All water, a decree has been passed against you. YOU HAVE TAKEN THE LIFE OF AN INNOCENT!" The thunder began to crack even louder. "For this we render PUNISHMENT. Mermaid is placed in dominion over you and all your children alike!" The ocean raging like a hurricane calmly replied. "Man cannot master the sea, nor can mortals move me." The thunder cracked so loud this time; glass cracked on ships hundreds of miles away. "SHE IS NOW MERMAID, GODESS OF THE OCEAN! ET IS done!"

FIRST TREE, THEN MOUNTAIN

 When they landed, they could not see the tops of the trees. A species humanoid but not human. Even with their advanced transhumanism enhanced sight, they could not see the tops of the trees. The magnitude and sheer girth of the trees was awe inspiring. This species had never seen trees before. They traveled thousands of light years to get to earth. "They", had technology far beyond human capability. A Species half human, half robotics, and no soul. The Deecyfs are a very destructive race that hides behind the guise of helping others. The Universe granted permission, for the Deecyfs to land upon earth. There was only one requirement made from the Universe. The Deecyfs had to go back in time. They could only visit earth a million years ago. The mission was deemed scientific. Thus, given permission to bring back samples.

Machine sounds could be heard clicking and whistling. The readings on their optic enhancers were going haywire. The Deecyfs did not have trees on their black heart planet. They had never seen a tree up close. Even then, they saw trees from present day earth. The trees they now viewed were from a million years ago. Giant trees standing over 2500 feet tall. Trees with trunks a square mile in diameter. These trees were ancient spirits millions of years old. Trees that were alive and central to the earth's temporal peace. The Scientists began climbing the giant trees. Crafts began to hover and take off towards the treetops. Climbing the giant mystical trees gave the climber a spiritual awakening. The Deecyfs did not have a soul but could still experience emotion. Climbing the magical trees gave the climbers sight beyond sight.

The tops of the giant trees were bigger than a city block. Crafts easily landed on the giant tree's branches. Everyone's recollection of the landing was different. The climbers' visions differentiated from the flyers. Those who flew to the tops of the giant trees could see far indeed. The climbers, on the other hand, could see sight within sight. The ones who climbed the giant trees could see past the South Pole. They could see past the ice wall to land masses. Land masses that most present-day humans do not even know exist. These ancient spirits were Moor than trees. They were forgotten gods.

The ground shook as the mighty trees angered in protest. The scientists were taking their samples. This angered the giant trees ferociously. The ancient spirits with weapons, were awoken. The ancient trees worked in unison. They began to shed their bark, fruit, and limbs. This caused massive destruction and loss of life. Tree branches the size of giant Sequoias crashed to the ground from half a mile up. This massive show of force crippled the scientist. They were not prepared for this. Most of their crafts and supplies were destroyed. There was only one thing to do. RETREAT!

FIRST TREE, THEN MOUTAINS AGAIN

The star system of the Deecyfs was devoid and bleak. These planet jumpers had manipulated all the neighboring planets inhabitants. The Deecyfs were ritualistic in their deceptions. A species of cowards unless they held the upper hand. Their tools were divisive and deceptive, yet simple. The Deecyfs preyed upon instability. Instability is their god! They waited, watched, and monitored for certain patterns. The patterns they were looking for were generational. Every species in the Universe has a hierarchy. The Deecyfs studied their neighboring planets inhabitants. Scourging other planets surfaces for their perceivable lower cast. Again, their method was simple. The Deecyfs ingratiated their selves as saviors. When in all actuality they prayed upon the offspring of the less fortunate. Profiting from the help they provided. "When one's help comes at a price, is "it" really help?"

The Deecyfs returned home with less than 1/3^{rd of} their team. Only 42 percent of their mission was viable. The only thing that kept the scientists from being executed were the samples they had retrieved. Samples that contained the fabled "God Spark." Transhumanism has its cost. Their god spark evaporated when they added machines to their organic bodies. The Deecyfs galaxy had been stripped dry of the god spark by them. Their neighboring galaxies were much too strong for them to take advantage of. Traveling thousands of light years using loopholes to steal life force was their main means of survival. Thus, the samples they retrieved were of the utmost importance.

"Ambassador Scurvy, what is your recommendation? What is the best sequence of events to obtain the god spark in the giant trees?" "Lord Asinine, we have found a chink in the giant trees armor. The giant trees are connected to their planet on an extremely intimate level. We have devised a plan to weaken the planet. When the planet has become weakened the giant trees will become feeble and vulnerable." "What is the percentage of success Ambassador Scurvy? Mind you Scurvy, be exactly accurate. Your continued existence depends upon it." "Of course, Lord Asinine. We have discovered a thick, rich, and dark colored substance inside of the earth. This substance, we believe, is the Life Blood of the planet. Earth is 0ver seventy-five percent water, a giant bowl with a diamond encasing. We will harness this oil substance from the veins of earth. Then we will intentionally release the oil substance into the earth's mighty oceans and seas. The earth is alive and has an engine. We believe releasing this substance into the earth's water will force the planet's engine to strain and struggle. The giant trees will feel this strain and struggle. This will make them emotionally vulnerable. We will lay seize upon the giant trees at their weakest moments."

FIRST TREE, NOW MOUTAINS

The Deecyfs returned to earth with crafts the size of Florida. Crafts capable of doing things humans would never be able to achieve. These crafts had three gargantuan tasks for which they were well equipped. Firstly, harnessing the oil substance and releasing "it" into the oceans. Next, they would use anatomic fissure to separate the giant trees from earth. Once the giant trees were separated from earth, they themselves would be harnessed as well.

There was a mighty ROAR, when the First Tree fell upon the surface of the earth. The planet began to vibrate as Mother Earth prepared to destroy the intruders. But, alas, there was no retaliation. Mother earth was weakened from the draining of her life force. Her life force had been released into her soul. This counter reacted to the earth's internal core. In turn, her engine was barely able to stay running. Mother Earth called upon her giant reptilians to help fend off the intruders. The Deecyfs quickly made the dinosaurs an extinct species. One by one the giant trees began to fall. Mother Earths soul moaned in anguish. The Deecyfs are heartless, soulless, they felt nothing for the giant trees.

The Deecyfs saved the mother of all trees for last. This First Tree, as they had deemed it, held the most life forces. The other giant trees only held one ancient spirit. This First Tree held at least two. The god spark in the mother tree was immeasurable. Even with their immense technology they could not calculate just what was in the First Tree. The Deecyfs held their inaugural god spark ritual. In the moonlight Ambassador Scurvy began to speak. "We are the many that pray upon the few. We are the species that manipulates and feeds upon the feeble. The meek are our substance." The chanting and humming began. The Deecyfs felt so semblance of emotion. In their vile heartless mechanics of bodies, they felt greed and ego. Ambassador Scurvy continued his spectacle of a speech.

"We will sever this First Tree and consume the sustenance and God spark thereof. We think you Great Aturn for the ability to project our reality upon this planet. Let not Our Order be hidden. We think you for this bounty as we consume The First Tree." A great flash ensued as the anatomic laser sliced through the first tree. Then "it" was done!

There was just one problem. The First Tree held in its trunk the "final defense." Long after the Deecyfs returned to wince they came from; something came out of the First Trees' trunk. The Deecyfs left some observers on the planet. These observers were to remain in the shadows. These observers were to remain on earth in hopes of the giant trees returning. The Deecyfs were meticulous in their observations and calculations. Although, there was one thing unbeknownst to them, Soul. Whatever "Et" was that came out of the First Tree, began to feed on the offspring of the Deecyfs. Thus, the natural balance of the planet began to restore herself.

A millennium had passed and Man with its technology were still fools. Repeating the same abuse to earth as the Deecyfs before them had done. Man built their giant structures and remembered not the giant trees. Such a sad remarkable sight. All the signs were before them. Yet they could not see what they did not know. Man could not tell the difference between the First Tree stumps and the Mountains. CC THE DEVILS TOWER! (Wyoming)

THE VISCOUS LADY BUG

_In a long way, Steppa was explaining "The Code of The Streets" to Snipe. "Do you know how hard it is to go from a ball to a cutey? Its rhetorical, do not answer." Snipe looked at Steppa intently. Trying his best not to laugh. Steppa continued. "Say you pay 125 for the ball. Now off dat ball, you might cut 3 hunnit." Snipes face lit up. He loved to hear his ninja speak on profit. He remained quiet. Focusing all his energy on not smiling. "Now you cut 300 and you think you are doing something right? Nah, don't work like dat. Off dat 3 hunnit you probably gonna make 250 max. But it is not really 250. One twenty-five goes back to the re-up. Now you have some decisions to make. Tell me Snipe, what would you do?"

"On Gang! First off, I'm a get me a bag. Not too much, know what I'm talking about, like a dub. Den I'm a shoot my bm 50. Put 20 in da tank. Den yop up me some wraps so I can twist one up." "Wow Snipe, you are a genius. No wonder every couple of days you're out here tryna rob something to get back on. Snipe, there's a code to this way of life. And a karmic debt to be paid. Instead of hitting a lick, then making a quick flip, you're hustling backwards." Now Snipe was not holding back a laugh anymore. In his mind Sh^t had just got real. Steppa had just insulted him. Snipe was not quite sure how to take it. He had his own code to the streets. Disrespect was not tolerated. It was met with force and eliminated. Steppa continued.

"Let me explain what I mean by hustling backwards. Snipe, you hitting a lick like a jack boy, then turning around spending the money like you some hellified huslta. Each day is not promised to you Snipe. When you plug dat clip into the belly of dat yopper, then use that energy as an ends to a mean; you better pray that energy doesn't come back on you with multiplication." "Well, WTF am I supposed to do Step? This is all we have. We have both been on the streets since jits! All this Cap! Taking the moral high ground right Steppa? The sad thing is you just hit a lick 6 months ago. What makes you so different from me?"

"There is an enormous difference Snipe. Just look at who I robbed. Who did I rob?" Finally, Snipe could not hold it in anymore. He broke out laughing at the thought of Steppas move he had bust. "You robbed StackO." "Snipe, do you even know why I robbed him?" "Come on Step don't try me like dat. Dude was from cross town. If you had not, I would've. He had "it" coming." "Wrong again Snipe. I robbed StakO cuz he made a play on our block. That was a training moment. I thought I was teaching you a valuable life lesson. Do you even remember what I said to him before I yopped em?" "Yeah. You said, "You can keep dat lil bit of paper but its gone cost you your life. BANG!" "Now, run your memory back Snipe. Did you see me go in StakO pockets and get his fiti?" "Nope!" "That is what I'm telling you Snipe. That was an example that was being made." Steppa continued to explain.

"StackO was neck deep in the game. This is what he signed up for. Snipe, soon as you pick up that first sack of rocks and start flipping it; your karma has begun. StakO was not innocent. Now let's talk about what you did last week Snipe." "Lol, what did I do Detective lol Steppa? Dis sh^t Crayola bruh." "Snipe, you robbed an everyday joe. A man that had a job and a family. A poor soul who just got money out the atm. He was on the way to get groceries for his family. You cannot see the difference in that? What you did was weak and cowardice. Even now, the "Streets" are watching your every move. Live by the gun, die by the gun. Display piss poor morals your life will be shortened." "I wonder where she puts the bodies?" "Oh wow! I gave you a 30-minute lecture on street codes and ethics, and you worried about old lady DoeBoe?"

Old lady DoeBoe lived across the street from the block Steppa and Snipe trapped/hustled on. Hustling provided Snipe with a lot of free time to watch Ms. DoeBoe. Whenever the block was too hot, Snipe always watched Ms. DoeBoe. He was so sure a pattern was there. The old lady had everyone fooled. Such a crafty witch Ms. DoeBoe is. Ms. DoeBoe had so many visitors. Some of her visitors brought bags. Others left with bags. The funny thing was, Ms. DoeBoe never left the house. The block Steppa and Snipe hustled on was one of the busiest in the city. Snipe was thinking to himself. "So much traffic here. Why would a little old lady live here in the middle of this.?"

THE VISCOUS LADY BUG STEPS BACK

Agent Square laid in his bed with one singular thought controlling every fiber of his existence. "Who Am I?" Agent Square was a walking contradiction. A good man with a bad job. He thought to himself, "Am I a bad man? My job is legal. But why do I feel so dirty sometimes?" Families were being broken apart and controlled. Although agent Square was not doing the breaking, he was aware of his part. The agency used Agent Square as an instrument to control families. Agent Square rationalized his position with the agency as best he could. The agent pondered on the ramifications of his action from the past week. Two children were removed from an abusive father. This helped him sleep a little at night but not much. Agent Square did not report the abuse because he had not seen any. Another agency alerted Agent Square to the change in status of the family he was monitoring. Working closely with the family for over a year, he had not seen the abuse alleged. When he submitted his notes, he had a good feeling in his heart. Then when the final report came out, there was no mention of his notes. This kept Agent Square up at night.

Agent Square started his day just as any other. He was eating a pulled pork sandwich and washing it down with milk. After washing his dishes, the agent grabbed his keys and headed to the office. Walking in the office he headed straight for his desk. Agent Square looked for his task folder and could not find it. His task folder was right on top of his desk. Usually, his task load was insurmountable to say the least. However, today was different, his task folder contained only one task. A child was reported missing over a year ago. Agent Square had the dubious task of informing the grandmother that there were no new leads. This infuriated Agent

Square. The old lady lived in the slums and did not even have a phone. He had an hour drive across the county to an environment that only a beast could love.

  The part of his job he hated most was upon him. Agent Square was on the way to the slums. His heart began to beat fast, and his hands started sweating profusely. He headed back to his house. He would take his gun with him. The last time in that neighborhood he had been robbed at gunpoint. He found himself out of gas and out of luck. The gas station he pulled up at only accepted cash. The atm machine was outside of the store. This neighborhood was so crime ridden that access to the store was denied. Every transaction at the store took place behind one-foot-thick bullet proof glass. Agent Square shuddered at the memory in his head. Remembering the robbery so vividly in his mental memory castle. He had withdrawn his money and turned around to see a scrawny teenager holding a hand cannon. The teenager had not said a word. He just pointed the gun at the agents' foot and pulled the trigger.

  The teenager had missed the agents' foot, but the damage had been done. The deafening sound of the gunshot reverberated through his spine as he remembered that horrifying day. He was so embarrassed thinking about the laughter that had begun after the shot was fired. The teenager had not hit him. Merely shot beside his foot. The hand cannon was so powerful that concrete ricocheted up and hit his ankle. This ricochet had forced a scream from Agent Square. The agent had fallen to the ground clutching his ankle and begging not to get shot again. This is what brought the laughter on. As the bystanders laughed hysterically, Agent Square continued pleading for his life. Begging not to be shot again. Only he had not gotten shot. The teenager picked up the money that had been tossed on the ground. Then said, "Nice pants dawg. You got good taste. Let me get them too. Take em off NOW! Or you won't even hear the next shot!" While taking off his pants the agent realized he hadn't been shot. The humiliation. The laughter. Agent Square cocked his Glock 40 and said, "Not This Time!"

Agent Square hated his last name. The children at his school had been merciless in his torment. Children could be so devilishly smart when goaded. The only memory Agent Square had from high school was a sickening one. A crushing punchline that cut straight to his bones when he heard Et. "Why would we let you in our friend circle? Bruh, you a SQUARE!" This joke was still being spread around the school even though the agent had graduated five years ago. Whenever the agent had a child client from his old high school, they always asked the same question. "Mr. Square? The Mr. Square? Like did you graduate from City High?" The agent did not see himself as a square. Far from it. He turned his radio up as he entered the slums. C-Murder was beating so hard that his rearview mirror was shaking. Agent Square cracked his windows so his music could be heard. C-Murder was snapping like a turtle. "Fu^k them otha Naggas. I'm down for My Naggas. Agent Square was Turnt! He had channeled his fear into anticipation. He was ready to get active.

Agent Square slipped the 40-caliber pistol in his pocket. He popped out of his vehicle with a smile on his face. C-Murder is still booming in his head. The Agent was looking for smoke. He had his mind made up. If anyone approached him that he viewed as a threat, he would fire a warning shot of his own. The Agency would understand. They were the ones that had encouraged him to get a gun. As the agent approached Ms. BoeDoes' door, he spotted the teenager who had robbed him the month before. The clouds blew away from the first quarter moon. Agent Square would have his revenge after all. The teenager crossed the street towards Agent Square with his hands held high above his head. Agent Square thought this was very odd. The teenager yelled out to Agent Square, "Aye My Nig, do not go in that house!" Agent Square removed his pistol. Held it straight up in the air and fired his warning shot. Ms.

DoeBoe, standing at the door stepped Back. The teenager laughed.
Then backed away with a mischievous look on his face.

<u>THE VISCOUS LADY BUG REVELATIONS</u>

Agent Square was so Amped up! The rush, the thrill of it all. He had
drawn his weapon, ripped off a shot in the slums and was still alive.
The agent was so enthralled in the euphoric moment he had
forgotten why he was in the slums to begin with. Now his thoughts
were, "Damn! Nobody is going to believe me. The single dopest day
of my life and not a single witness. Like, WTF! Why me? But of
course, there were a thousand people around when I got robbed.
Everybody with all their social media tags. They even made a meme
out of me." The agent chuckled to himself. The meme they made of
him was funny. In fact, when he first saw the meme, he laughed at
himself. The meme was video of him handing over his pants with
the audio silent. Instead of the actual audio it was a song playing
instead. Eightball and MJG, Smooth Armed Robbery. "Just like
Picasso, I had to paint a picture." Epic. Agent Square was so caught
up in his daydreams that when he turned around to knock on the
door, Ms. DoeBoe scared him. Ms. DoeBoe was standing less than a
foot away from the agent when he turned around. The old lady,
being short and hunchbacked, was not in the agent's vision. The
agent turned around, took a half of a step, and then bumped into
Ms. DoeBoe. Agent Square screamed and jumped up in the air
simultaneously. He screamed so loud that people thought he was a
human chicken getting his neck wrung.

Agent Square landed, slipped, and almost fell again. He clutched at
his heart and had a dumb look on his face. "What the HELL IS
WRONG WITH YOU LADY!" "Hello, my darling little aphid. Please, oh
do come in. Won't you come in out of the dark and cold little

Tommy?" If someone had walked up to Agent Square and asked him if this lil ole lady freaked him out, he would have said FAX! Not facts but Big FAX! Ms. DoeBoe gave him the creeps. He knew what an aphid was but who the hell was Tommy? Ms. DoeBoe continued, "I have such delicious stuff in the fridge Tommy. Tommy, are you out there?" Agents Squares skin began to crawl. There was something extremely effed with this ole lady. "Calling me Tommy and I got this 40 cal on me." He continued to think to himself, "Man, I'll shoot the sh^t out you your old ass lady. You do not know me like dat. In this neighborhood, sneaking up behind people. Ok, I'll be Tommy. Your old ass better have something good in here to eat." "Yes Ms. DoeBoe, Tommy is coming in to eat."

  "Hello, my little aphid, such a deliciously sweat boy." Now Agent Square was starting to get freaked out. The agent placed his hand inside his jacket pocket. The affirmation of the Glocks plastic gave him cause to relax a bit. 'Tommy, the food is in the refrigerator. Take whatever you like. Agent Square smiled and thought to himself in a sarcastic tone, "Lol, this bish is like whoa." The agent calmly turned and opened the fridge. He took a peak in and then closed the fridge. Quickly looking back at the old lady, as if trying to catch her doing something. Tommy, she called out, "Tommy, do you know why I call you Tommy?" Agent Square mumbled under his voice, "I don't give a f^ck." 'What did you say Tommy?" The agent answered, "I said no, please tell me." Agent Square turned and opened the fridge. To his surprise the old lady had a feast in her fridge. Ms. DoeBoe continued, "Tommy is a code word." Agent Square was not paying much attention to her at all really.

  "Yes Ms. DoeBoe, that's great, it really is." By this point, Agent Square was stuffing rolls in his mouth. Ms. DoeBoe, a four-foot two-inch old lady, let her garbs fall to the ground. The old lady continued, "Yes, my little aphid. Tommy is code for Deecyfs! Tommy you are a direct descendant of the intruders who tore away the ancient ones!" The agent, now stuffing his mouth full of cinnamon swirls replied, "Yep, again, that's great news." Ms. DoeBoe stretched her legs and extended herself to full height. She pulled off her skin suit to reveal a ladybug. This was no normal ladybug; Ms. DoeBoe now stood close to seven feet tall. Ms. DoeBoe let out a wicked snarl and then spoke. "Feels so good to have that skin suit off and stretch my legs!" Agent Square dropped the glass of milk out of his hand. The jar fell and shattered. The old lady's voice had left him paralyzed for a couple seconds. Then he remembered the Glock again. The agent smiled and then turned to face her.

   Puma peered down from the roof trusts of Ms. DoeBoes house. He had been slipping in and out of Ms. DoeBoes' house for a week undetected. Looking down at the monstrosity before him, Puma only felt puzzlement. He was not puzzled by the ladybug as much as he was by her previous form. The whole week previous, Puma had been feeling DeJa'Vu. Just where in the hell had he seen this old lady?

   Puma had an earpiece attached to his ear. Although he could not speak in his cat form, he could listen and understand. Agent Swim began to speak. "This is it, Puma. We do not know if it is the guy that just walked in or the old lady. All we know is the energy signal reported last half-moon is in that house. IDGAD which one of those creeps is demonic! Kill em both Soldier. Swim out! Agent Swim switched to radio silence. Beethoven's 16th quartet began to play through Puma's earpiece. It was time! Puma and Agent Swim would make their beautiful MUSIC!

   As Puma began to descend upon them, something happened. The man had turned around, let out a frightful scream and dropped his gun. The Viscous Ladybug disappeared and then reappeared latched to the man's face. Now Puma had solved the puzzle. This was the old lady that had taken the boy with the pendant. The old lady that had cursed him.

The Viscous Ladybug bit into Agent Squares head. The agent's head burst like a melon. His brain matter splattered the walls. Puma now stood in the old lady's kitchen. Standing in his boy form. Ms. DoeBoe had sucked Agent Square bone dry. He looked like a giant headless grape. The Viscous Ladybug discarded the body. Then put her skin suit back on, being fully aware of Puma patiently waiting. The old lady began to croak out her witch sounding words. "The hokshila and the pendant. What took you so long?" Puma tersely replied, "Order of the Hidden!" Agent Mermaid Swim, not wanting to be left out, chimed in two words of her own...

"WENDELL ETERNAL"

MY TIME IS NOW!

YOUTUBE HANDLE

MEDITATION HIDDEN WISDOM

https://youtu.be/ht6Aje4VFAo

SPECIAL THANKS TO

TASHAPIATHACHO

MY MOTHER

MY GRANDMOTHERS

MY DAUGHTERS

MY FATHER

WAKAN TAKAN

AMMA AND ABBA

WENDELL ETERNAL

Volume II

ORDER OF THE HIDDEN

"If you take your child to a battlefield, do not cry out to god when that child dies."

THE SUCCESSFUL BUSINESS MAN

The lights are off, but someone is home. The town veterinarian, Timmy S, is up scheming. Doc was not his preferred nickname, that's just what everyone called him. Doc had gotten tired of trying to correct people. Plus, his wife and daughter did not think Timmy S. was cool at all. They thought it was stupid. Little did they know, Doc was a successful businessperson masquerading as a town vet. Sure, he had graduated college and was a legal vet but that was not his heart's desire. Doc wanted to help animals. Once he realized euthanasia was forty-two percent of his practice, his heart changed from good to diabolical.

Ninety-four percent of the time, Docs' Day started off the same. He would wake up to a quiet house. Once Docs feet hit the wood floor in his bedroom, all hell would break lose. Teazer, his blue nose Pitbull, would make a mad dash to his harness. The harness was located 6 feet in the air on a small shelf. Teazer would sit under that shelf with the meanest, most intimidating look a dog could muster. This perfectly trained masterpiece of a dog would patiently set still just like a statue. Teazer, waiting on the leader of the pack, would watch the steps like a hawk. When Doc came down the steps, the two old friends would just look intently at each other. Until Doc spoke.

 "What's up Teazer, you want to go for a run?" "BARK, BARK!" Teazer would bark Hell Yeah! Then he would jump up and grab his harness. After he grabbed his harness, he would sling it over to Doc. Then, Teazer would pat his feet and wag his tail. Walking his dog everyday not only strengthened their bond but had increased Teaser's intelligence. This was no ordinary walk in the park. Doc was in damn great shape. This was no walk; this was a race. Doc slipped the harness on Teazer and then snapped on the 10-foot leash. The two adversaries headed to the back yard towards the alley. Teazer did not pull Doc, he walked calmly beside him. The two sprinters got to the alley, and it was Time!

 Doc was fast, super-fast. The two took off! Rocks flying everywhere. The first 20 yards, Teazer always played possum. By the time they got to 40 yards, Teazer was smoking Doc. When Teazer began to pull Doc, he always released the leash. Teazer would then kick into another gear and leave his adversary in the dust. Teazer was so far ahead of Doc, he could barely see him. Then out of the corner of his eye, Doc saw something beside him. Doc slowed a bit and looked to his left. Judge, the massive lab-rottweiler mix, was chasing him. Doc was already gassed. He was running full speed for over 100 yards. Judge caught up to him, barked, then lunged at Doc. Doc let out a scream and jumped straight up into the air. By the time he landed, Teazer pulled up, and he was Pissed!

 This two-hundred-pound monster was getting his ass handed to him. Teazer, this 79-pound pit, had Moor game in him than a PS6. It was like watching a puma fight a tiger. Only the puma was just as strong and much faster. Teazer forced Judge back into his own yard. If judge had been any smaller, he would have already been dead. Doc screamed at Teazer, "Stop boy! Stop! Come on, let's go home." When this did not work, the only thing Doc could think of was to sprint towards his house and say, "Bye Teazer!" Teazer finally let up. He barked

a couple of times as if to say, "Your Lucky pal."
Then he followed Doc home.

THE SUCCESSFUL BUSINESS MAN Goes Vegan

  Part one of Docs two-fold plan had come to fruition. The town vet was now the proud owner of the only buffet restaurant in town. Not just any restaurant. The newly renamed "Almost Vegan Buffet." "One of a kind menu," was Doc's motto. The only meat on the menu was chicken. Everything else was exotic fruits and veggies from all over the world. The special of the day never changed but the town loved it. With the purchase of an adult meal, children 13 and under had free access to the giant salad bar. All the fruits and vegetables they could eat. The chicken was on the other side of the restaurant and had an attendant. If you were 17 and under, you had to be accompanied by an adult. It was a risk hiring the attendant, but it had paid off. The profits increased 20 percent once the attendant started checking for ids.

Part two of Docs ultimate plan was proving to be a bit Moor difficult. The town vet had already switched over to vegan soon as the buffet opened. Most people thought this was a gimmick. Doc ran radio ads saying, "The Mega Salad Bar Made Me Do "it!" When people asked him what is "it"? Doc would say, "Go Vegan!" Doc had his own reasons for going vegan and it was not a gimmick. He wanted his wife and daughter to go vegan too. Doc had explained to his wife, "Honey, come on, you've got to see the profit in this?" To which she replied, "I had an exciting and fulfilling career. I took a desk job to help you run this restaurant. Now you want to tell me it was all to get me to go vegan. Please be incredibly careful how you answer this dear." Timmy S. had seen that look in her eyes before. The Doc knew his wife could get active if she was angry. People did not last long if they got on her bad side.

"Ok, new approach," the Doc thought to himself. "That was a dead end. I am just going to have to go facts on her." Mery loved her facts. The same way his wife could intimidate him with her icy cold stare, he could do with facts. Mery could not help herself when presented with cold hard facts. That is what made their bond so strong. Doc would never argue with her. If it were important enough, he would merely present her with facts. This was a lovely game of cat and mouse they both enjoyed. The Docs job was to get as many facts as possible into his wife before she caught on to what he was doing. If she caught on right away, he would lose, and she would not be interested in playing, "The Game." He would have to wait a couple of weeks.

"Hey Mery, did you hear about that restaurant that has been closed for two years? It's on the other side of town." "No Honey, what about it?" "It is for sale. The owners are tied up in court and lawsuits for the past three years. I'm thinking a second "Almost Vegan", would put us on the map. You know, like a tourist attraction." "So, who is going to run this, Tim? You're pissing me OFF! I did not sign up for this Sh*t!" "That's the beauty. With a second location we can both retire. I've crunched the numbers." Doc slid over a folder to his wife. "FACTS!" That's the word that went through Doc's head as he passed Mery the folder. Her beloved facts. These numbers were not fudged in any way. Thus, making that folder he just slid her, "Facts!"

Mery's eyes lit up. Doc was thinking to himself. "That's it, that's it, just a little bit more." The game was unfolding, this was the moment he had been waiting for. If Mery asked him a question about the numbers, then she would be interested. While she was interested, he could then hit her with moor facts. Like the real hidden fact, he wanted to share with her. Mery continued to read as a slight smile started to crack in the corner of her mouth. Mery thought to herself. "Ok, he has got me. He took the time to prepare all this just so I could ask him a question. After I ask my question, he's going to tell me what he really wants to say. I could easily win right now. Just throw the paper aside and walk off. But I do want to get out of this damn restaurant business. "

Mery read another page and a half. Then she finally gave in. She could see that Doc had spent months on this report. Plus, Mery had a question to ask, and she wanted an immediate answer. "Ok Tim, you win. I see you drew up this fancy report with all this detail. So, I'm assuming you left the time frame and start date off intentionally." Doc replied, "I did." "Ok Tim, if I let you buy your restaurant how long will it be before we can retire?" "Assuming we get her up and running in 6 months; I would say about 18 months after that. So, lets say 2 to 3 years max."

 This made Mery excited. She was super stoaked! She was hoping and praying. Five years or less. He had said two to three years. She was having a challenging time controlling herself. If she acted too happy, Doc would never let her hear the end of it. Mery said, "I guess that could work." "Girl Stop!" Doc was laughing hard now. He knew he had won. His wives' words had come out one way, but her face told a different story. When Mery said, "I guess that will work," she had bitten down on her bottom lip and looked a way." Even with her head turned, Doc could see her smiling. "Mery, turn around and look at me. I want to see if you're happy." She couldn't take it anymore. Mery burst out laughing. "Damn "it" Tim! I'm mad at you. You got me. Ok, you win. What the hell is it that you want?"

This was Tim's chance. He could not rush it. He had to slide smoothly. "Oh, nothing. Do you want to go there and see it? Babe, it is in great shape." Mery looked at her husband with a quizzical look. She was confused. She had not counted on that. Mery thought to herself, "Just what the hell is he up to?" "Sure Hun, when do you want to go?" Doc knew his wife inside and out. He studied her. He knew what all her facial expression meant. Doc had seen that look on her face before. He had her. She really did not know what the hell he was up to. My time is NOW! He answered his wife, "We can go tomorrow morning. We got a steal on this place Mery. The owners are losing their asses in court. Want to know what they are charged with?" "What?" "Well, it seems they got caught with a whole bunch of small tools used for preparing cats and dogs. Just, what in the hell is this world coming too? I'm glad I'm vegan." Mery's mouth dropped open. Her gum fell out of her mouth. That was her and her daughter's favorite restaurant before it got shut down.

Now, Mery's face was bright purple. She was angry. She was not mad at her husband; she was mad at herself. He had totally duped her. This was his intent the whole time. Mery thought to herself, "He did all of this, just to get us to go vegan." He had presented her with the facts, the cold hard facts. Now Mery knew her, and her daughter had been eating cat and dog three years ago when Tommy's was open. Now Doc swung the hammer and pushed the final nail into her stance on meat. He did not need facts now. He had touched her heart. So, he continued to go the emotional route. Doc said, "Hey babe, could you imagine if someone had stolen Teazer as a pup and……." "Just stop. Ok, ok, I get the point. Vegan we are."

THE SUCCESSFUL BUSINESS MAN, JOB WELL DONE

Twenty-four months later Timmy S. was feeling good. No one called him Doc anymore. The "Almost Vegan II" had been wildly successful. The town vet wasn't a vet anymore. He was a successful businessperson to the fullest extent. Doc was hardly ever at his office anymore. He hired another vet to do the heavy lifting for him. Doc would just over see the euthanasia and safe disposals.

The Doc wasn't having second thoughts, he just hated the waste. He thought to himself how hard he had worked to get here. Now, he was just going to give it away. The sell was final, money had already changed hands. Doc thought to himself, "I really did "it". I fooled them all."

Mery had already purchased tickets to the Swiss Alps and updated their passports. The "Town Vet" inside him had died. The Malcolm "By any Means necessary" route, had worked. This new man, Timmy S., had taken his shot and hit. Not only had he hit once, but he had also hit twice. Timmy S. thought to himself, 'Yeah, it is time. Cash out and dip. Plus, the wife would get me killed if I even asked her about another business endeavor."

Their plane was departing Saturday. This would be the last night the trio would spend at the restaurant. Doc's daughter was sad. She loved the place. Mery was ecstatic, ready to travel the world again. Just one quick little meeting with Skimp and he was out. Skimp was Docs insider. His scammer. Skimp managed all the food processing info. The companies that provided the products and the payments. Doc had a going away present for Skimp. Skimp had originally been pissed that his easy mill ticket was ending. Doc would give him 100 racks to smooth things over. Skimp asked to meet Doc at the restaurant. Skimp had a surprise for the doc too.

Skimp walked in with the Sheriff. He looked around, spotted Timmy S. and waved. The Doc did not wave back. A dozen moor men shot into the restaurant. THE GIG WAS UP! Skimp was caught with meth two weeks ago and decided that he would not take his 10, he would just tell on a friend. Instead of taking ten years for the meth; he snitched on the doctor.

Mery was amazingly calm. Normally she would have flashed her high security badge by now.

Instead, she just patiently watched, trying to see why Tim was looking so dumbfounded.

Instead of properly disposing of the animals he euthanized, The Doc had been mixing it with his chicken. It had been easy. The only meat he served was chicken. Their number one bestselling item was a mix of dog, cat, and chicken. The Sheriff walked up to Doc. Mery came and stood right beside him. The Sheriff spoke. "Dr. Timothy Swim, turn around and place your hands behind your back." The Sheriff began to read off Dr. Swims charges and Mery did not even bat an eye. She was no longer Mery. That cold steal stare had returned. She was Agent Mermaid Swim.

The Sheriff cuffed the successful businessman and began to lead him to the car personally. He had a few choice words for his long-time friend. "Doc, how could you? You have scarred my daughter and the rest of this town's children for life. My little Maggie loves those damn Pup Nuggets. She is still going to be asking for them. Then when she finds out...." Dr. Swim cut the Sheriff off. "I never gave them anything. It was you and her mother who showed id to get to those Pup Nuggets. So, all I can say Sheriff is, Job Well Done!"

<u>BRACKISH WATER, WALKING LIZARD</u>

"Folks, you don't want to miss this! The 11th annual Lizard Water Walking Races! We've got the best Basilisk lizards in the known Universe. Now folks, last year's top price took home twenty-five thousand dollars. This is a three-day event. The final race will be one hundred dollars a ticket. We support our military and……" Matt changed the channel. "Damn ads!" "Matty, are we almost there yet?" "Are we there yet? I told you to stop calling me Matty. It's not funny anymore. Now, it is just annoying." "Maybe I wouldn't call you Matty if you took us on a real vacation." "Trish, this is a real vacation, I'm paying real money for "it"." No Matty, I don't want to see lizard's race. Three days of you drunk watching lizards walk on water, fun meter is 0!" "Will first off, this is a gambling venture. And secondly…."

It was too late. Trish had already put her earphones in and let her seat back. She was going to be in a bitchy mood this weekend and he deserved it. Matt thought to himself, "Why did I buy ten 100 -dollar tickets? When Trish finds out I am dead meat. Unless....one of them hits!"

The water was perfectly still and calm. Lake StarWess was the perfect setting for the race. Camp StarWess was a huge attraction for one weekend out of the year. People from all over the state came to see the water walking lizard's race. It was like a spring break festival but only for gamblers and hunters. The oddest arrangement and assortment of people that you could imagine. Add alcohol and gambling and you've got a volatile and fun environment.

The sweat heart water picnic was on Friday night and the races would start Saturday at first sun light. "Babe, do you want to go to the sweat heart water picnic tonight?" Trish thought to herself, "God why? Could this possibly get any worse?" Then she replied, "What happed to your hound staking the rabbit thing you wanted to go to?" "Trish, why do you have to be so cynical? It's called "Hound Rabbit Stakes" it's a race." "Because it sounds like cruelty to animals Matty. And if you're cruel to the animals, the animals will be cruel to you!" Matt wasn't listening. He was thinking about his tickets for the race on Sunday. "So, ma, you wanna go or not?" "Yes, Mathew Adam the III, I will go got damn it! Just stop me by the liquor store first!" Trish did not want to go to a water picnic at night with a bunch of hunters all around the lake. The whole thing seemed dumb to her. The only thought she had running through her mind was, "I can't stand his Ass!"

  Welp, she was right. This had been the worse night of her life. Literally! Bugs biting, make up running and Matt drunk. Matt pulled a fast one on her. He told her he would go in and get her drinks. Matt got her some wine coolers and himself 10 miniatures of fireball. By the time Trish realized he was drunk, he only had three bottles left. "I'm ready to go back to the room MATT!" Matt burst out laughing and almost fell off the boat. "Oh, but wait, what happened to Matty?" Matt burst out laughing again.

  Lake StarWess was huge. Trish and Matt were a 45-minute boat ride back to the boat doc. The less secluded side, they now found themselves on, had a floating store. Matt got a 12 pack of beer and some smokes. He stopped before getting back on the boat. "Damn girl, you are fine as f^ck." Trish fake smiled and then flipped him off. 'Well, what the heck was dat for?" "You're drunk Matt!" 'I'm not drunk Trishy! I'm crashing. I got beer to level me out. I could see if I had got more liquor. Damn Debbie Downer."

Three hours later, Trish was fast asleep, and Matt was even more drunk. The lake was a lot bigger than he thought. All the boat ramps looked the same in the dark. The pontoon was getting harder to navigate. Matt steered towards a huge log that was halfway in the water. He dropped anchor and could tell he was only in four to five feet of water. Matt peed on the log and started collecting all his beer bottles. After he gathered the beer bottles, he tried to toss them on the other side of the log. But he missed!

Instead, the bottles had smashed violently onto the log. "Why you little mother f^cker!" Matt was terrified. The voice he heard sounded like the boogey man. He was wondering if he had rifles aimed at him for littering. The folks in Camp

StarWess were dead serious about littering. Matt timidly replied, "Whose there, what's going on? "SPLASH!" Matt didn't hear the splash, he felt it! A giant tail had smacked him across his chest and knocked him into the water. Trish woke up just in time to see the log move. Only, this was not a log. This was a massive saltwater crocodile.

 Another big splash. Trish screamed! She called out to Matt. "Matt, Matt!" Then she spotted him. Trish felt so relieved. He looked hurt but at least he was alive. "Matt, get over here, come on!" Matt did not move or reply. Trish had mascara in her eyes, she could not see clearly. She cleared her eyes and squinted in the pitch-black dark of the lake water. Trish grabbed the light and flashed it on Matt. What she saw would haunt her for the rest of her life. Matt was bitten clean in half from the waist up. His belt buckles reflected light back at Trish. Matts feet were still twitching before they began to sink. Trish began to scream again.

BRACKISH WATER, ALLIGATOR

"Chief, I'm telling you, this was not an alligator."
"Why Earl? Just because you've hunted and trapped here your whole life?" "It's not that Chief. I'm telling you; the bites just don't match up." "The bites just don't match up? So now you're the authority on gators? What the hell difference does it make anyway? Crocodile or alligator? We will find it and kill "it"." "Chief, we haven't pulled a gator out of this water in ten years. That was a 12-footer. That gator was the county record." "Earl, please get to the point. What are you really trying to say?" "The crocodile that did this is at least 20 feet long."

Chief Hemmingway went back to his house and twisted one up. He took a couple of tokes and turned-on YouTube. The Chief started thinking about what Earl said, then a video caught his eye. "Effects of Weed and Dairy on The Melanin."

(By Da13thsun) https://youtu.be/lPdpcXF3uJo

Then he switched to a lesser-known creator, "Meditation Hidden Wisdom." This guy was a nut. He had all these different types of videos. One video In particular caught the attention of the

Chief. The video was a one-minute YouTube short. It was a clip from "The Game of Thrones." Danny was telling her dragon Drogon, to burn the masters. This made the Chief think about what Earl had said. "The crocodile that did this is at least 20 feet long." Chief Hemmingway shuddered at the thought of a real-life dragon being right in the center of Camp StarWess.

   The Vibe at Camp StarWess went from hype to somber overnight. The Chief had tried to keep it a secret, but Trish was a stubborn girl. Had the Chief told her to tell as many people as possible, she would have told no one. Be that as it may, Chief Hemingway had asked Trish to tell no one. In respect for the family. Trish had agreed not to say anything. Partly because she didn't know what to say and because she was still in shock. The next day, while Trish was setting in her room waiting for Matts family to arrive; she watched the news. When the news anchor said it had been a 10-to-12-foot alligator who attacked Matt, a chill went down her spine. Trish had been trying her best not to re-think or re-live any of "it." She just blocked all thoughts of the savage attack out of her head.

After watching the news, she could not help herself. Trish was now rethinking what happened.

 Trish was fast asleep when she heard Matt say, "Whose there." Then she heard a massive SPLASH! When she stood up on the pontoon, she had saw a dragon. Even now as she re-thought what happened fear gripped her, and she let out a yelp. Trish was no herpetologist, but she knew the difference between 10 feet and 20. Trish called the news station and told her story. This changed everything. Pandemonium had struck.

 The mayor of Camp StarWess had called Chief Hemingway and told him the cold hard facts. Mayor KeenWits exact words..." There's no way in Hell we are canceling this weekend and refunding all those damn tickets!" This sparked a visceral conversation between the mayor and the chief. "Lives mayor, we're talking about lives!" "No Chief Hemingway we are not talking lives. We're talking about your job! This city runs on this one weekend. Get out there and find that damn Gator!"

 "Funny thing about crocodiles is, they can go a long time without eating." Chief Hemingway then replied, "Earl, are you stupid or just plain old dumb? There are thousands of people on this water right now. At any minute someone could die. But you still must constantly say crocodile this and crocodile that. Please, Earl, just give it a rest!"

BRACKISH WATER, HUMAN WALKER

 Earl was right. A croc could go long periods between meals. Lol, if it wanted to. The Salty struck again. This giant saltwater croc, that everyone was told was a gator, struck again! This time the unthinkable happened. Mayor Keenwit was basking in the sun right by the water's edge. The mayor looked at the water and thought to himself, "Damn fools. They believe anything the news tells em. This water aint even safe enough for a dog." The mayor then let out a chuckle. That's the moment everything went horribly wrong. "Go get it girl, go get it!" The mayor screamed "NOOOOO!" Time slowed down as the mayor turned around. What he saw made his stomach sink. Tyler, the mayor's nephew had just thrown Dreems toy football into the lake.

Tyler was stone cold drunk. He had forgotten all about the gator talk. Plus, it was all kinds of boats on the water. Tyler was state champ, and he was celebrating. He just received his acceptance letter from Noter Dame. Even though he was drunk, his arm wasn't. He flung Dreems toy football so hard; the dog couldn't even see where it landed. Dreem, a female Cocker spaniel, had the most beautiful curly black hair. This dog loved to swim but she was a stubborn bitch. No pun intended. Once Dreem hit that water, she would not come back until she got her toy.

Mayor Keenwit screamed NOOOO! It was too late. The Cocker Spaniel had taken off like a bullet. Dreem was swimming like a fish. Tyler was looking at his uncle and laughing. Tyler couldn't understand why the mayor looked so damn sad and serious. "Dreem, Dreem. Treat, Treat. I've got treat, treat." Then the mayor screamed "Dreem!" By this time, Tyler was beside himself. He was rolling on the ground holding his stomach laughing. Laughing so hard tears were coming down his face. Mayor Keenwit stood by the water's edge with his hoarse voice.

The mayor couldn't even scream anymore. Now his calls were a mere whimper. Dreem had not even made it to her toy yet. Then, that's when "it" happened. Sal, the giant saltwater croc, struck again. Sal swam in behind Dreem. Putting himself between the dog and land. Then he started thrashing about to make a spectacle for the people. The mayor saw the splashing of the 20-foot croc and took a step away from the water. He was no longer calling for his dog. He was in shock! Dreem had almost made it to her toy when Sal swallowed her whole. The massive croc didn't even slow down. His huge mouth just opened, and the dog and toy went in. Mayor Keenwit didn't have to give any money back, but he had lost his best friend. This pained him greatly and he declared war on the giant croc.

The weekend was a success. The mayor did not have to refund the tickets and there were no moor fatalities. Sure, Matts family had threatened a civil suit, but he'd pay them off later. Mayor Keenwit had bigger fish to fry. Well, not fish but you get the point. Earl, the game warden, and Dr. Yolan met in the mayor's office early Monday morning. Dr. Yolan, the most tenured Herpetologist in the state, was breaking down the dilemma. Dr. Yolan went on to explain, "Lake StarWess is around ten square miles in circumference. There are two smaller streams feeding into Lake StarWess. These two streams bring in saltwater from the ocean. This raises the salinity level of Lake StarWess. Making the water brackish for the most part. This brackish……" The mayor interrupted. "I don't need a science lesson doctor. How do we kill "it"?"

Dr. Yolan shot the mayor a glance and then continued as if he hadn't heard the mayor's comment. "This brackish water has provided enough salinity to sustain this prehistoric beast. We are going to have to disrupt its habitat and force him up one of these two streams." Earl then interjected. "Well, what if we do disrupt his habitat and he doesn't go up either of these streams? What if he decides to swim through the swamp?" "Don't be ridiculous Earl. This time of year, that swamp is only about a foot deep. There is no way in hell this massive croc could traverse five miles through less than a foot of water and mud." "Ok doc let us say he does. What is are recourse?" "Well, that's simple Earl, that's what we have you for. An animal this size would leave a trail so massive even a child could follow. Also, it would take at least 24 hours for him to get to the other body of water. If not longer."

Lake StarWess was a massive body of water. The good thing was that it wasn't that deep. Only 50 feet deep in most places. A croc this size would need sunlight in the morning to regain energy from the cooler night. Two ships were configured with nets. These nets had five-foot square openings in them, to allow other aquatic marine life to pass through. Dr. Yolan devised a device that would directly affect the auditory sensitivity of reptiles. Two ships dredged the lake with nets while thirteen smaller boats blasted sonar. Hunters and trappers from all over the state volunteered for a chance to shoot this present-day dinosaur.

The stage was set. The hunters and trappers surveyed the lakes' edges looking for the croc. Two ships dredged the lake with their massive 100-yard nets. Both streams had patrols eagerly waiting for the croc to try and swim upstream to the ocean. The sonar blasted as the marine life in Lake StarWess went crazy. There was only one problem.

Sal, the saltwater crocodile was no crocodile. Sal was a man masquerading as a crocodile. This giant crocodile was once a man. A man who had made a deal with the devil. Sal had been granted Eternal life and great power. The devil had obliged. Transforming Sal into a giant saltwater crocodile in the process. A saltwater crocodile that could walk on two feet like a man. Sunday night Sal simply walked through the swamp to the next body of water.

BEAUTIFUL MUSIC

_Just as Puma raised the Pendant above his head, the Viscous Ladybug disappeared. She reappeared where Puma had been. Puma narrowly darting away. He bounced off her refrigerator knocking it down. Landing on her bed he let out a ROAR! Beethoven's 16 Quartet played in Puma's ear. Agent Swims voice buzzed in. "Steady now soldier. Rember the plan is to get her outside, so we can hit her with the heavy artillery." Puma glanced at the door. Then sprung for the opening. The ladybug disappeared then reappeared at the door.

The two collided into each other. Puma getting bit in the chest. Then managing to smack one of the ladybugs eyes clean out of the socket. The viscous ladybug Howled! In her most sinister voice, the ladybug spoke. "I'll be in your nightmares hokshila. Then Ms. DoeBoe turned into a beautiful ladybug. She flew right out the window. Puma roared as the Viscous Ladybug escaped beyond his reach.

BEAUTIFUL MUSIC GNIK AND MEARD

Meard- Where you at?

Gnik- Where I'm at?

Meard- Bruh, don't play.

Gnik- Hold on lil momma. Let me go head an chin check dis sh^t right now! Now listen, I'm not gonna be out here eating and beating any otha cat. But if you think you gonna put down on me or boss me around…. GIRL…you done bumped yo got damn head!

Meard- FINE!

NARARATOR- Meard hangs up the phone. Gnik has just picked Meard up, she has just sat down in the car.

Meard- Where are we going!

Gnik- Well got damn…. you still mad?

Meard- why would I have anything to be mad about?

Gnik- Idk. I'm assuming you are. Cuz you aint say hi or try and lean in for a kiss. Do you even know if I smell like another chic or not?

Meard- Pull the car over now! Let me out!

Gnik- Lol. We are going to the facility. And please stop wit da madness. Like…you literally mad, cuz I'm not gonna let you play with my head.

Meard- What you did was way more messed up!

Gnik- How in the hell is that?

Meard- You made a sex clip and sent it to me! Who does that? What the F^ck kind of time you on bruh!?

Gnik- Nagga, you were out of the state for months. Ok, dats cool. Then you pump fake like we are getting back together. Then you sleep with some dude you are calling your X. But you met him after you met me. Dat math don't math. Make it make sense.

Meard- I'm not going to be able to get that clip out of my head.

Gnik- That's good. Because you are not going to be able to beat me. You might have seen a weaker side of me. Crying about my children or over my sick mother. But if you think I won't break a bish down like pound…. you sleep.

Meard- Fine! Why are we going to the facility?

NARARATOR- Gnik doesn't say a word. He calmly pulls the car over and gets out. Opens up Meards door and takes her by the hand. He pulls her out and gives her a big hug and a kiss. They both get back in the car.

Gnik- Were picking up a subject.

Meard- Wow! So, you lied? You said vacation. This is freaking work sounding to me.

Gnik- "It" is work but it's also a vacation.

Meard- How so?

Gnik- This particular subject needs a vacation.

Meard- Which subject is Et?

Gnik- Girl you know I can't tell you dat.

Meard- Please just tell me. You tell me everything and you know I'm not gonna stop asking. Is "it" Negro?

Meard- YES! Don't ask me sh^t else about this! Just be happy we fixn to be Glamping or whatever da hell you said last week.

NARARATOR- Gnik and Meard arrive at Fort Tashapiathacho. A place with inconceivable beauty in abundance. Two enormous bodies of water and a swamp. Beautiful streams and trees everywhere. With cave systems connecting to the mountains. Five square miles of forest carved in between two mountains. Fort Tasha is a no hunting zone with nature walking freely all around you. Each cabin has 5 acres of land for seclusion. Every cabin comes with 5-star amenities.

Meard- Ok, I take "it" back. This might be nice.

Gnik- Yah think? Just wait to you see inside.

NARARATOR- Gnik and Meard park. Before they go inside Gnik starts the timer to unlock the subject. Once the subject finished his vacation he would return. Gnik would then get an alert.

Gnik- Ok, close your eyes.

Meard- Do I have too?

Gnik- Girl close your eyes.

Gnik- Ok, you can open them now. Tadaah!!!

Meard- WOW! This is mad dope! How much was this?

Gnik- "It" was free. It's free for two days only, perk from the facility.

Meard- Two days? That's not a long-time babe.

Gnik- Girl, you can't sit your hot ass still for two minutes. I'm sure two days will be plenty fine. So, what do you want to do?

Meard- We need to go to the grocery store.

Gnik- Oh wow, you did that on purpose. You knew we had to get groceries before we came all the way up the mountain. Yet, you let me forget.

Meard- So what. I wanted to see the cabin. I've seen the cabin and now I'm in a great mood. But if you keep complaining, I can get bitchey. Do you really want that?

Gnik- No mam. You win. Nough said. Let's go get the groceries.

BEAUTIFUL MUSIC BONDING

Gnik- So who is cooking tonight? Me or you?

Meard- I am silly. What do you want?

NARARATOR- Gniks face lit up like he was a kid in a candy store.

Gnik- Well, in that case, I think I want a....

Meard- Hold up, pause. Just so you know, if you want this big extravagant meal, I'm probably going to be too tired to fool around later.

Gnik- Damn! That's a hell of a decision. Your body or your cooking. I'm going to need a min to think this over.

Meard- Well, if you have to think about "it", I think you should just get neither.

Gnik- That's exactly why we make such a great team. Because I don't let you do the thinking for me. Now, let me see. I think I want some black bean burgers. Oh, and some of your homemade banana vegan ice cream too. And then….

NARARATOR- Meard is just looking at Gnik with her eye browns contorted. Trying to figure out if Gnik is serious or not.

Gnik- And then we can go to that little adult store that we saw on the way down the mountain. You can get whatever you like. Then later, I can chit chat dat chinchilla. Give you that feeling that you like so much. You know the one. The one where you can't feel your legs?

Meard- There is a word to describe you but I just cant think of it now. How many other girls have you used that line on?

Gnik- Don't matter. You like it. When I said, "Chit chat dat chinchilla", you started smiling. So, stop the shenanigans.

NARARATOR- The two life partners leave the grocery store and head to Tempest X to pick up some toys. They pick up some toys and head back to the cabin. After they eat, they go on a long walk around the property. They take a shower. Party like rock stars and then the pillow talk starts.

Meard- This is the best night ever. It's making me a little sad though.

Gnik- Why?

Meard- When we leave here, we have to go back to the grind. This place is so magical. Why do people have to work?

Gnik- That's simple. People are lazy and idle hands are the devil's workshop. The people that can control their passions and impulses can use their mind to generate currency. When you get to a certain level spiritually, you will never work a day in your life again.

Meard- How is that?

Gnik- When you connect to your higher self, you have a higher inner standing of yourself. When you truly know who you are, you can then maximize the gifts the CREATORS gave you.

Meard- What gifts? Like, gifts don't pay bills. Money does.

Gnik- Well what about your writing? I think it's dope!

Meard- Yeah but you said I would probably have to sell my soul to be a bestselling author.

Gnik- That's not exactly what I said. I said If you want to be famous in this world, you must give up the universe.

Meard- I don't understand. What's the difference?

Gnik- You can manifest yourself to be extremely fortunate. In this way you can have fortune without fame.

Meard- Well, how do I manifest myself to fortune?

Gnik-Sacrifice! Everything comes with a price.

Meard- Are you saying what I think you're saying?

Gnik- There are many forms of sacrifice. Some chose humans and animals. The people who practice human and animal sacrifices are looking outside of themselves for validation. They are operating on a very low frequency/vibration. Yes, the magic they wield is powerful, but it comes with a price. To gain world renown on this planet you must give up the universe. Once you sign a soul contract you can never leave this planet. Because you will be agreeing to turn a blind eye to the plight of the human race.

Meard- Dats deep. But what are some other types of sacrifices?

Gnik- The most powerful sacrifice I practice is fasting. Everyone has a destructive habit that they do, even though they know it's bad for them. If you abstain and fast during prayer and or deep meditation, your manifestations come true rapidly and abundantly.

Meard- So what do you think about...

Gnik- Girl stop stalling. Is you ready for round two or not?

Meard- Why not, we're already naked anyways.

BEAUTIFUL MUSIC ANCIENT

Powerful footsteps can be heard trampling through the forest. The birds chirping stops. The owls aren't hooting. Something is amiss. The powerful thud of feet creeping through the forest is getting louder. Puma is twenty-five feet in the air, sleeping on a tree limb. When Puma awakes, he's instantly alert. He's got a weird feeling. Puma thinks to himself, "What is this feeling?" The footsteps grow louder and get closer. Pumas' spine tingles and the fur on the back of his neck is raised. "Just what the hell is this feeling?"

Then Et happens! Pumas' cat eyes spot a walking monster, a dragon. The enormous monster walks right under the limb he is perched on. Puma realizes what this feeling is. ITS FEAR! The massive monstrosity walks right by Puma. Puma is thinking to himself, "This is abnormal. Outside of nature.

I've got to do something!" Frozen in fear, Puma can't move a muscle. The sheer size and girth of this monster has frightened Puma. The Enormous monster continued walking through the forest. Unimpeded by the one thing that could stop him.

 An hour passed before Puma slinked down the tree. The scent left by this monster was unmistakable. Puma did not have his earpiece in. He was supposed to be on vacation, whatever the hell that was. Puma decided he would track the creature. Whenever the creature decided to take cover, Puma would report back to Agent Swim. After about four miles, the scent lead Puma to the kennel he was released from. Puma darted into the cabin.

 Inside the cabin was a scene likened to a battlefield. To the untrained eye "it" would look like a war had taken place. That's not what happened at all. The monster had crashed in through the bedroom wall. Taken Gnik and Meard by surprise. Still, the two highly trained agents had let off over a hundred rounds. The two agents had Glocks with silencers on them. No big guns. They were not hunters, they were guards. Puma let out a loud ROAR! The only thing left was blood. The monster had not only killed them, but he had also eaten the remains.

Pumas' fear was replaced with rage. Now he was not tracking the monster, he was in hot pursuit. Bouncing and darting through the wooded area, Puma let out a mighty Roar! His fear had cost him dearly. Meard and Gnik were his friends. Although they did not have much direct contact with each other. Gnik had picked out this beautiful place and told Puma he needed a vacation. Meard had always called Puma negro because of his black fur. Meard had lost her life because of his fear. The fear left. There was only rage.

Puma finally tracked him down. He roared as the massive monster slowed down and then turned to face him. Sal let out a chuckle. Puma and Sal were eye to eye, merely 13 feet apart. Sal continued to laugh and then said. "Coward! I smelt your scent hours ago. I was so close to you I could taste you.

Coward! You sat somewhere perfectly still. I bet you didn't even move a whisker." Puma roared massively. Sal, the Saltwater crocodile continued to laugh. "No matter. I love eating cat for dessert anyways!" The massive croc now stood up on his back legs and continued to laugh. "You tracked me for a reason. Now let's get on with "it"!"

Puma looked up at the massive croc standing nearly 20 feet tall. He calculated in his head that he could easily jump up to the crocs head. But then what? Puma roared again and flexed his claws out. He thought to himself, "I could never win this fight. Even still I will surely die. This will be a good death. I would rather die on my claws than live with the shame of fear." Puma took a couple of bounces and then shot straight up into the air. Right before he made contact with Sal, his pendant was removed. Puma was now the boy. Time stood still as my ancient ancestor appeared to him. Mary Molly aka Tashapiathacho called out to Puma. "Keysari." Puma was in a daze. He did not respond.

"Keysari." Puma recognized the name, but it was not his own. He had heard that name before. Et was familiar to him but why? This time in a more intimate and loving tone, the ancient ancestor spoke again. "Keysari." Puma now realized why he knew that name. Keysari was the name of The Boy and The Pendant. Keysari was Puma in human form. Puma answered. "Yes." "Keysari, why do you sacrifice your life in this manner? This is a battle that you cannot physically win?"

The boy replied, "I will win. I must!" "Yes, you have lost many and suffered greatly in your lifetime. Your time is Now! The wrongs will be righted. I will see to that. My blood is your blood. Our blood is one. Your present actions will bring your life force to an end. Et is not your time to die. I will grant you the power of a Siberian Tiger. The largest of all living big cats. This monster will die, but not today." Puma woke up on a tree limb with Beethoven's 25th quartet Moonlight Sonata, playing in his mind.

THE STORY OF A MAN

Jhonny called out to the children. "ROAD TRIP!" Three sets of feet slammed down on the mahogany wood floors. The boys were up and ready. Jhonny and his wife April were taking the boys to the country. This was no pitter patter of feet. This was a stampede! The boys raced each other to the steps. Each one wanting to make "it" to their dad first, so they could ask where the road trip was to. Jhonny Jr., the oldest, was first down the steps. The twins, Jason and Jimmy, were fast on his trail. Even though Jhonny Jr. was 13, he had his hands full with the twins. The twins worked together instinctively as one.

Just as Jhonny Jr. was in full sprint, the heavens collapsed. Jason, the oldest of the twins, dropped his bedspread and pillows down on Jhonny Jr. Jhonny Jr. tripped and fell with the bedspread over his head and the pillows breaking his fall. Jimmy jumped over his older brother and shouted, "Lil

Jit!" Jhonny Jr. being seven years older than his brothers, always called them lil jits. Jason shouted down from the banister to his older brother, "Gang, Gang, Twin Gang!" Jhonny Jr. laid on the floor with his arms crossed. He wasn't even angry. He loved his little brothers. Jhonny Jr. considered himself a knife and his brothers were the sharpening stone.

Jimmy slid up to his father and shouted, "Twin Gang!" Jhonny Sr. and his son did the patented Salvator handshake. "Where are we going dad?" "You and your brother go get the bedspread off JJ. Help him up and then I'll tell y'all together. I'm all for Twin Gang and big brother competition but y'all cheated and he could have gotten hurt." Jason, now shooting into the kitchen said, "Did we get him? Where are we going?" Jimmy replied to Jason, "Dad said we cheated. We need to help JJ up." The twins helped their brother up and the three of them walked into the kitchen together.

"April, get off that darn phone. Lets tell the boys where we are going." April hung the phone up and walked into the kitchen. Jhonny Sr. began to speak. "Ok boys, we are going to Trim Tree Creek!"

Jhonny Jr. repeated what his dad said, "Trim Tree Creek?" The twins began to shout, "TRIM TREE CREEK, TRIM TREE CREEK!" Jhonny Jr. had a puzzled look on his face. Then he said, "Dad, where is Trim Tree Creek?" Jhonny Sr. just smiled at his son and said. "Go get ready." The twins continued chanting, "Trim Tree Creek, Trim Tree Creek!"

The twins were still chanting Trim Tree Creek when they pulled up at their father's office. JJ, the oldest of the boys said, "Dad, why are we at your office?" Jhonny Sr. replied to his son, "This is not an office. This is a way of life. Today, I teach you boys that way of life." The twins stopped chanting and Jason said, "Hey, wait a minute. What's going on?" April looked at her husband and said, "Yeah dad, what's going on?" Jhonny Sr. thought to himself, "Got damn that women is a traitor. She knows good and got damn well what's going on. We talked about this last night. Now she is playing dumb so the boys will just be mad at me for trying to teach them the family business."

"Today is the day I teach you young men the family business. There is a creek in the back of the office. I'm going to teach you how to trim trees." JJ became angry because he had figured out what the twins had not. JJ spurted out, "You lied to us dad?" "No son, I did not. I told you we are going to Trim Tree Creek. There is a creek as I've just told you and we will be trimming trees." Now the twins had figured out what was going on. Jimmy shouted out to his father, "This sucks dad!" Jason looked at his mother. His mother just looked away. April knew the boys needed to be taught responsibility. Tricking "her boys" like this angered her. She hated the way Jhonny manipulated them like this.

   All and all, et was a pretty productive day. The twins played in the creek all day. Jhonny and JJ had trimmed the trees and had a good time. April stayed on the phone in between playing with the twins. JJ asked his father a lot of questions. The boy had really taken an interest in the family business. Not so much the work aspect but the numbers. "How much did you say you make a week dad?" Jhonny Sr. replied, "Well son, I make about 3 k a week." "And how much did you say I'll be making when I start collaborating with you?" "I don't know JJ. Depends on how good you are. If you start helping now and training, by the time you're 16, I'll give you 16 an hour." "That doesn't sound like much. Is that a lot dad?" "Sure it is JJ, sure it is."

JJ helped his father carry the twins in. He wanted to talk to his father more about the numbers. JJ loved numbers. "Ok dad, so you said you gross 3 k a week, right? What happens after that?" "Well Junior, after that is a thing called Net. I must pay workers compensation, insurance, and taxes." "Well then, how much is left after that?" "Around 2 k." "Ok, ok. And how much is mom's net?" "Well, your mom makes a little bit more than me. She makes around 2300 a week net." "Wow, mom makes 1200 more than you a month! Twelve-hundred dollars more a month doesn't sound like a little bit dad. And if it's only a little bit more, can I have 1200 dollars for my birthday then?"

<u>THE STORY OF A MAN, FATHERSHIP</u>

"It" was the 9th of April, but "it" felt like summer. The boys were sleep and Jhonny Sr. had just awoken from a cat nap. The four of them had played touch football from breakfast to lunch. Every Sunday for two years this had been a tradition. Normally Jhonny Sr. and the boys slept for an hour or two. Today Jhonny Sr. woke up after only about fifteen minutes. He wasn't comfortable. His back was hurting, and he needed to stretch. Jhonny Sr. got up and decided to go check on his wife. And again, she was on the phone.

  As Jhonny Sr. came down the steps, he heard his wife talking. Not wanting to ease drop on her conversation, he decided to announce himself. "April! Who you talking to ma?" April yelped. He had caught her by surprise. She just hung the phone up and said, "Jen." "Jen", Jhonny thought to himself. "That doesn't make sense. Jen went to the south pole to see the land beyond the ice wall." Even though Jen was his wife's friend, Jhonny knew more about her comings and goings then his wife did. Summer came early this year. It was April but everything was growing rapidly. Jen was Johnny's' customer. Jen had given Jhonny explicit instructions for her fruit trees. She said she would be gone for several months and would have no cell service.

Jhonny decided to dig a little deeper. Jen had given him all these instructions just two days ago. There was no way she was back already. There were only two possible scenarios. Jen had not gone on her trip or April was lying. "So, what did she say ma? Is she really enjoying her trip to the Bahamas?" April stiffened a little bit, her heart beating out of her chest. "Yeah babe, she loves it." Jhonny felt a ping in his heart. That ping then grew to an ache. She had lied. April had lied. She wasn't talking to Jen. Then who the hell was she talking to?

Jhonny decided to go Debo. He would ask her for her phone. If she said no, he would take her phone. April had never lied before. Why now? "Aye babe, funny thing is, Jen is not in the Bahamas. She is at the south pole. Did you forget she has been my customer for the last three months?" Now the beating in April's heart was a pounding action. Her stomach began to knot up. This was "it". The thing she had feared all this time. Pandoras Box was now open! April did not reply. She just turned around to face her husband. Soon as they made eye contact, Jhonny knew.

 "How long?" The tears began to roll down April's face. She was not sad she had gotten caught. No, these were tears of relief. The lie was over. It was truth telling time. Jhonny Sr. called out to his wife again. "How long?" She could lie no more. The truth cut like a Yoda light saber. "Thirteen years!" 'Wtf! So, you started an affair right after Junior was born?" "JJ is turning 14 next week. That well make "it" 14 years." There, she had said it. Hopefully, her husband had caught the truth of the matter. Now tears started rolling down Johnny's face. "So, Junior isn't Junior?" April did love Jhonny and it hurt her to hurt him. No matter, she had to speak her truth. "Jhonny, I begged you not to name him after you. You would not listen."

 And there "it" was, The cold hard facts. Jhonny had more questions, but he feared the answers. Tears rolled down his face moor rapidly now. He went upstairs and looked at his boys. Wondering if at least the twins were his. But too scared to ask April. Jhonny went to the master bedroom and began to pack his things. He hurt so bad, he wanted to fall on the floor in a fetal position and cry his heart out. There was still one question he wanted an answer to.

Jhonny went downstairs with his bags packed and sat them down. He walked into the kitchen. His wife was sitting at the table with a blank stare on her face. Jhonny summoned up the strength for a chuckle. He looked at his wife and said, "Thanks ma, I mean for the honesty. I just have one question. I don't even want to know why. I just need to know the who? Who is he?" April was in shock. She thought she would feel better after telling him her secret. Now all she felt was pain for the boys. For all of them. "April! I said, who is He!" April blinked a couple of times and then kept up with the honesty. "Vegas!"

Now everything all made sense. Jhonny and April got married 20 years ago. They had tried to have children for several years. Then all of the sudden, April had gotten a new job and then pregnant soon after. April had begged Jhonny for five years to come to the fertility doctor with her. Jhonny never went with her because he did not want children. It was only after Jhonny Jr. was born, that Jhonny now loved children.

Jhonny repeated what his wife said. "VEGAS!" Do you mean your boss? Your boss Vegas?" April had a stoic look on her face. She simply replied, "Yes Jhonny. Vegas my boss." Now something snapped in Jhonny. The tears dried up and the pain in his gut was gone. Vegas and his wife Karen had always been extra, they had always done the most. Throughout her job at the accounting agency, April had kept receiving raises and vacation days. Any time they would go on vacation, Vegas and Karen would always watch the boys for them.

Now the true plot had unfolded. They had played Jhonny like a loose fiddle on Sunday at the poor folk's blues bar. Jhonny had a smirk on his face as he looked at his wife. He turned, walked right past his bags, and left the house.

THE STORY OF A MANS SOUL

The last two months had gone horribly for Johnny, but he didn't seem to care. Jhonny had moved out of the house and left it to April and the boys. One day, when he came by to visit, the door was unlocked, and all the furniture was gone. The only thing in the house was a note on the back of the door. The note read, "Sorry Jhonny, I just can't anymore. The boys and I are moving upstate." Jhonny read the letter, crumpled it up and calmly walked out of the house. Four weeks after that, Jhonny had not heard from April or the boys. He did not even know where they were.

Exactly four weeks after April and the boys moved, Jhonny got a letter in the mail. It was DNA results. He calmly opened the results. He read them and found out that the twins were not his either. Jhonny crumpled up the letter, smiled and then turned the tv on. He finished watching his favorite show and then went upstairs to pack his toolbox. Only two words were running through Jhonny's head "Road Trip!"

Just as Jhonny arrived at his motel, he was struck with an epiphany. His favorite movie was "Officer and Gentlemen." Jhonny walked into the little motel with a reenactment on his mind. He paid for his room and then said, "Watch this!" Jhonny took his wedding ring off and then swallowed it. The motel clerk said, "Here is your key weirdo." Jhonny just smiled and said, "You don't even know the half bro." He took the key from the clerk and started singing. "Love lift us up where we belong!" While Jhonny was exiting the motel lobby, the clerk repeated the same word again, "Weirdo!"

Jhonny was ready to make his deal with the devil. Good or bad. Did not matter, he was willing to live with "IT". He walked out of his motel room with toolbox in hand and a great smile on his face. Jhonny had recently liquidated his assets and bought a new car. He had a bright red Charger RT with the Hemi engine. He thought to himself, "This damn thing is loud." Jhonny hopped in the car and pushed the start button. The Hemi engine began to purr like a tiger who was about to be let out of a cage. He put her in reverse, then in drive and tore off. All you heard was the screeching of tires as the Charger got sideways.

Jhonny turned on his music. His favorite song was locked into repeat. It was Sade, "Hang on to your love." Sade had just said his favorite line, "Why are you walking away? Why do you play these games?" When he looked in the rearview mirror, Jhonny saw smoke and black tire marks. He sped up the mountain with nerves of steel. He almost hoped he would kill himself, although that was not his mission. He was speeding up the mountain doing 100 miles an hour. The only way he could keep her on the road was to ride in the middle of the two-lane road.

If at any moment a car was coming down the mountain, there would be a horrible crash. "It" was inevitable, something would have to give. Either he would wreck, the other car would wreck, or they both would. Either way, the stakes were feisty and high. Jhonny approached the top of the mountain with his hemi roaring. There was only one driveway and one house. He revved up the engine a bit and pulled in the driveway. Jhonny got out of the car and grabbed his toolbox. He put on his shades and headed toward the front door. He rang the bell. With his dark glasses and palm-tree shirt on, no one even recognized him. The door was opened. When the child spoke to Jhonny, he patted him on the head and walked right by him.

 The child said, "Hey Mr., I did not say enter! Dad!" The child was hollering for his father while Jhonny walked into the kitchen. He said hello to the lady. The lady dropped her glass on the floor. The glass shattered. Jhonny opened his toolbox and took out his gun. The lady just froze, unable to move. Jhonny took off his glasses and said, "Hi April." He let two shots go and then said, "By April."

 Vegas had broken up with his wife Karen. He had come clean and told her the truth. Vegas, April, and the boys had moved upstate to a house on a mountain. They were going to have their happily ever after; or so they thought. What they did not count on was Jhonny and Karen wanting revenge. Karen felt just as much pain as Jhonny had, if not more. Karen found out where Jhonny lived and had come to his apartment one night. She had rung his bell with a big bottle of Hennessy in her arms. When Jhonny answered the door, Karen said, "I know where they're at. But you must promise me that you will kill them both!" Then she walked into Johnny's apartment.

Vegas heard the shots. He grabbed his gun and ran down the steps. He shoved the boys into the living room closet. Vegas cocked his snub nose 357 and was ready to get active. He walked into the room and was bewildered. April had blood everywhere and a man was lying on the floor with blood on his face. Vegas got a couple of feet closer with his gun pointed right at the intruder. It looked like the man had shot April and then taken his own life. Vegas took a peak over at April and then fell to the ground. He had not heard the shot that burst his brain open. Jhonny was playing possum. Soon as Vegas looked over at April, Jhonny shot him dead.

A year later, Jhonny Salvator was found guilty of murder in the first-degree times two. During his trial Karen had come to see him for the entire year. They had fallen in love. Jhonny had miscalculated. His favorite show was CSI. He figured he would only get 20 to 25 years since he did not premeditate the murders. Although, he did not premeditate his wife's murder, the jury found that he had premeditated April's lover Vegas's murder. Instead of getting 20 to 25 years, Jhonny was getting the chair. When sentencing was read, Karen screamed at the top of her lungs. She started hollering at the judge, "Do you know what they did to us!? They did this to themselves!!!" Karen had to be restrained and Jhonny was taken back to his holding cell.

Jhonny sat in his holding cell thinking to himself. Then he said aloud, "I'd give anything to be out of this cell and live a life with Karen." An old lady's creaky witch voice could be heard saying, "Anything?" Jhonny thought his mind was playing tricks on him. An old lady had just disappeared on one side of his holding cell. Then reappeared inside his holding cell. "Did you say anything boy?" Jhonny blinked a couple times and started smacking himself in the face and saying, "You're not real, You're not real!" When he opened his eyes again, he screamed. The woman had turned into a monster.

"I've come to collect your soul boy. You can die now, or you can barter with your soul." Jhonny screamed again and then urinated on himself. The

Viscous Lady bug he saw before him, had him terrified. He sputtered out a word. "B-b-b-arter?" The old lady began to speak. "Yes, you foolish boy. I have the power to grant you immortality and power beyond your wildest dreams." "And--- all.... You want is my soul?" The lady answered, "Yes, among other things, but for now let us start with your soul. Where you are going you would not need Et anyways." Jhonny had nothing to lose. He said "OK!" The old lady then said. "It" is done!"

Jhonny had great pain in his stomach, and he fell to the ground. The old lady began to laugh in an Erie gleeful way. Jhonny began to thrash about on the ground as his body began to swell and grow. Yelling and screaming, Jhonny tore at his flesh. The pain was unbearable, and the witch just kept watching and laughing.

Forty-two seconds later, the transformation had been completed. Jhonny could barely fit in his cell. Jhonny now had a monstrous voice. He called out to old lady DoeBoe, "What HAVE YOU DONE TO ME!" To which the old lady tersely replied, "Order of the Hidden!" The massive monster began to thrash around and burst out of his cell. The monster was running on two feet. Just as Sal, the saltwater croc approached LakeWess, he said two words, "Wendell Eternal!"

THANK YOU FOR YOUR TIME

WENDELL ETERNAL

3

ORDER OF THE HIDDEN

STARTED 7-24-23.

AHJANIQUE

KEYSARI SMOOTHIE

The funny thing about Agent Swim was her personality. She had this hilarious personality that she didn't even know she had. People would always laugh at her jokes. The problem was they were not jokes. Most of the times she was dead a^s serious. Puma explained everything to Agent Swim. All the gory details. Even the part about how he was struck by fear and couldn't move. Puma was finishing up his story when he saw Agents Swims' eyes begin to squint closed. Puma explained to her that this was not a physical fight he could win. That Sal was demonic, and bullets or weapons could not kill him. Agent Swim batted her eyes a couple of times, took a sip of her coffee and said, "I Hate Got Damn Mondays!" The room erupted in laughter. Just 3 minutes ago Agent Swim was bragging about Mondays. She said she loved them.

Puma did not sit long with his pride. After being free on vacation, the giant enclosure did not resemble a sanctuary any longer. Now this multi million dollar subterranean was just a gage in his eyes. The veil had been removed; he could see clearly. Tashapiathacho revealed something to him that he had not previously been aware of. That there are levels to this. There was no shame in being a mountain lion but being a human was an upgrade spiritually. That is if one took advantage of the gifts he or she was given.

Other shapeshifters were men or women who shifted to animals. Puma was different. A mountain lion that shifted to a boy. This gave Puma a totally different outlook. When a man shifts to an animal, he gives in to his animalistic urges. When an animal shifts to a man, that animal gives in to human nature. Having given in to that human nature, Puma's mind was running rampant with confused thoughts. He thought to himself, "Why would an ancient ancestor intercede with my life? Better yet why give me the strength of a Siberian Tiger for a battle I can't physically win?" So many questions he had that he needed answers to.

Pumas' thought process had totally shifted. Before he was an animal just trying to survive, who rarely stayed in human form for long. As he began to stay in his human form for more lengthy periods, raw red meat was not appealing to him any longer. Puma didn't bother to try cooked flesh. To him flesh was flesh. Something had to die for flesh to be made meat. Now with his human nature taking over life and death meant moor to him than sustenance. Puma fasted for two days. On the third day he remembered what Gnik and Meard used to start their days with. A smoothie!

Water alone was keeping him alive. Puma was very hungry after two days with no food. This feeling was a feeling that he knew. That he remembered from being a lion on a mountain. The hunger pains began to bang away at his gut while he read books on nutrition. Puma wanted to eat to live. He did not want to live to eat. Puma searched in his memory castle. Searching his mind for the time he spent with Gnik and Meard. Gnik and Meard were the ones that transported him from old lady DoeBoes house. Meard had broken all protocol and made Gnik stop at their house instead of the facility. When Puma shot into his encasement, he had left a trail of blood all over the concrete. The facility was over an hour away. Agent Swim and her men were swarming all over, looking for the viscous ladybug. They could not take Puma to a vet. He would of bleed out had Meard not sown him up.

  Gnik had rushed Puma into the house and placed him on the table. Meard had begun to clean and dress his wounds. They both worked frantically to save Puma's life. "It" seemed like they were oblivious to the fact they had a giant black puma on their table. That is until Meard had started sewing up Puma's chest and he let out a loud growl. Meard let out a loud Yelp! And then she froze. Gnik started laughing and then rubbed Pumas ears. Meard, remembering that Puma could understand her said, "Not Funny!" Then she continued to sew him up. They dressed Pumas wounds and then laid him on their couch. Then came the terrifying job of calling Agent Swim. Gnik paced back in fourth in the kitchen with the phone in his hand. Meard sat in a chair with a big smile on her face. Gnik stopped pacing, looked at her and said, "Alright, just what the hell is so damn funny? This is serious sh^t. We could be in a lot of trouble for this. Forget the jobs we could be terminated!"

  Meard covered her mouth and then looked away. Finally, she burst out laughing. Then she repeated what Gnik had said. "Terminated!" Then laughed some more. Now Gnik was pissed. He said, "So what is "it"? Do you have a death wish or something? So, you just don't care about dying or are you just doing this to piss me off?" Meard replied, "No, it's just so funny seeing you like this. You're always so gun hoe. So, Gang Gang. Remember we walked past those three douche bags on the west end? They stared at us so hard. I was scared and didn't have my piece. I asked you did you have yours and you said, "Don't need "it". When the fighting starts just call them an ambulance." Now look at you." Now Gnik was laughing. "You're a Jerk Meard!" Gnik stopped pacing and made the call to Agent Swim.

Agent Swim answered the phone with her steel voice. She did not say hello. She said, "This better be important!" Gnik said, "I had to bring the "subject" to location 1031." "Status report on the subject Agent G!" Gnik replied, "non-terminal and stable." "When the "subject" is ready for transport, enact flux 86 to location 1031." "Yes Mam."

Gnik hung up the phone and sat down. Now Meard was worried. She was scared to ask but couldn't help herself. "What did she say babe?" Gnik replied, "She said after Negro is ready for transport enact flux 86." Meard just had a quizzical look on her face. She had not been on the team long enough to even know what the hell that meant. Meard being a very intelligent woman knew what 86 meant. She however did not know what flux 86 was. Meard sat down, crossed her legs Indian style and took a couple of deep breaths. She slowed her breathing down and prepared her mind for what was to come. The first thing they taught at the agency is there is an afterlife, so don't be scared to die. The time had come for her to put that training to the test. Meard waited a couple MooR minuets and then said, "Ok, what the hell is flux 86?"

Gnik replied, "Its not actually flux 86. It's more like enact flux 86 to location 1031." Now Meards breathing began to pick up. Her heartbeat began to increase. A little droplet of sweat streaked down her right temple. Meard did not want to die. Running from the Agency would be suicide. She couldn't take "it" anymore. She finally blurted out, "Just What the F^ck is Up?!!" Gnik looked at Meard and then said, "Good news or bad news first?" Meard sat back in her chair and thought to herself. "Well at least we are not going to die, I don't think. But he did say bad news." "Ok, what is the bad news?" Gnik said, "We must set fire to the house and take only one small bag. So, get your coach bag and put your girl stuff in there." Meards suntanned face began to turn beat red. Meard and

Gnik had just finished moving into their new house. Meard shouted out, "No! We just moved into this Got Damned House! It's in the middle of nowhere! Agent Swim is just being a b6tch! Call her back and tell her No!"

 "First off calm down. Secondly, it's not Agent Swim in circumstances like this. Right now, she is Colonel Mermaid Swim, head of the Dark Weapons Protection Department." "Well, that's just great King! Really effn Great!" Meard knew breaking protocol was a terminatable offense. She didn't care and continued to use Gniks real name. "So, what's the good news King! What's the effn good news?!" Gnik opened the fridge and said, "I went grocery shopping last night. I got all the things for our smoothies. Kale, apples, squash, honey dew, black walnut and wormwood, apple cider vinegar, oatmeal, frozen banana and pineapple." And there "it" was. Puma had searched his memory castle and found his friend's smoothie recipe.

KEYSARI BACKTRACKS

 Agent Swim was beyond pissed. Most people outside of her inner circle did not know why she was so pissed. The Agency thought "it" was because she was losing her control. This was not the case at all. Agent Swim was pissed because she didn't want to lose Puma. When Puma informed her that he wanted to be called Keysari while in human form, her eyebrows furrowed. Then while Agent Swim was drinking her coffee, Keysari said, "Also, I need to go alone on this one. I've thought about what you said and still must go alone." Agent Swim stood up, and said, "OK!" Then she calmly walked over to the trash can and dropped her almost full cup of coffee in the container.

If Agent Swim was pissed before, now she was enraged. Keysari, growing Moor and Moor intelligent by the second, had out maneuvered her. As they sat in the black SUV, they didn't say much. Agent Swim transported Keysari back to Fort Tashapiathacho. Keysari knew better than to tell Agent Swim the full scope of his plan. He wanted to wait until they arrived at their destination. Once they exited the vehicles Keysari said, "Mery, I'm going to be here for a month. I will not break radio silence until the subject is rendered incapacitated. I will not be around any electronic devices nor need anything provided for me."

This is where the rage kicked in. Agent Swim walked over to Keysari and gave him a hug. Keysari noticed that tears were rolling down her cheeks under her dark sunglasses. As Keysari walked off towards the wooded area he heard a loud SLAM! Agent Swim had slammed her SUV door so hard the window had shattered. Keysari stopped and looked back at her. He wanted to go to her. Although he looked at her as a big sister, she looked at him as the son she never had. Agent Swim sat in her SUV deciding if she was going to leave or break her word and stay somewhere close anyways. Then she looked up and saw Keysari watching her. Her commander instincts took back over. Agent Swim took off her sunglasses and mouthed the words, "Go get him Tiger!" Keysari could not only hear her from 20 yards away, but he could read her lips as well. Now he had clarity of what Tashapiathacho meant when she said, "I will give you the strength of a Siberian Tiger." Not physical, metaphysical.

Keysari started the five mile walk to the cabin where Meard and Gnik had been murdered. As he began to trek deeper in the forested area, he could feel the dark energy encompassing him. There was not fear, merely an awareness that his life was indeed in eminent danger.

The birds were not chirping, instead they were singing songs. Those with spirit ears knew exactly what they were singing. They were singing a warning song. The song was a warning for all who entered the forest. Keysari could here the fear in their song. He knew all to well of the fear they had sung of. For Keysari himself had been terrified the night Sal had walked into the forest. A twenty-foot crocodile was nothing to laugh at. Now if you take that same twenty-foot crocodile and see him walking upright, it was terrifying to say the least. The birds chirping began to intensify as he approached the cabin where Gnik and Meard had met their demise. As Keysari approached the 5-acre lot the cabin was located on, he saw the yellow tape with the DWPD logo all over "it". The agency had taken control of the property and probably did a total wipe of all evidence.

As Keysari walked up to the property he saw the massive hole Sal had crashed through. His eyes began to glass up and fill with water. Blood was on his hands. He felt directly responsible for the deaths of his friends. His fear had rendered him helpless when he first felt the demonic energy of Sal. Keysari entered the cabin and immediately noticed it did not look the same as before. All the blood was gone now. All the bullet casings were removed. The furniture, although broken, was now back in its place. There was a deep feeling of despair in the cabin. Keysari even thought he heard crying ever so faintly. He walked through the cabin ever delicately not to disturb anything. He was looking for something. There "it" was. On the counter undisturbed by the destroyed cabin all around "it". He had located the blender. Fresh fruits and vegetables would be delivered just outside the yellow tape every 6 to 7 days. Keysari left the cabin and walked deeper into the forest.

Even after he had walked a mile away from the cabin, he could still hear the faintest of crying. Even though he was alone in the forest. The rabbits, deer and squirrels had fled the area. Now all that remained was the birds singing their sad songs. After a couple of hours Keysari located the spot where he and Sal had faced off. Once he got to that spot, that old feeling of fear started creeping up. The feeling started in his gut then rose to his chest. Keysari calmed himself and found a big tree. He laid down with his back against the tree and began to meditate. He had learned this from a YouTube video that he watched. Da13th Sun taught him that trees are ancient spirits and relieve stress and tension when you relax up against them. After about 30 minutes Keysari got into a deep meditative state. While in this deep meditative state Tashapiathacho appeared to him again.

"The brave warrior returns to right the wrongs., to bring back balance to this land." Keysari replied, "Yes, I have come. I will do what I must. I will continue to fight the good fight." Tasha said, "Be aware of your surroundings Keysari. There is on in this forest who will help you." Before he could ask her who, she was gone. Keysari awoke from his meditation feeling invigorated and refreshed. The fear had subsided, and he began to trek deeper into the forest. He searched his memory castle for some Beautiful Music. The tune that came to his head was none other than Antonio Vivaldi, Concerto in G minor, Op 8 number 2. He could no longer hear the birds singing nor the forest crying.

As night hit and the wind chilled Keysari removed his pendant. The black puma was here. He announced his presence by letting out a loud roar. He continued his mission searching for Sal, the giant salt-water crocodile. After hours of searching Keysari finally caught the scent he had been looking for. This was not a scent of crocodile. This was a scent of demonic energy. An unbridled care for nature and the balance there of. He did not rush through the forest. Keysari used precaution with every step he took. The trail went cold a couple of times, but the puma easily picked "it" up again. Sal was smart, he had been covering up his tracks. Keysari noted this in his memory castle. The trail led him to a small creek that was a little over twenty feet wide. Keysari sat at the edge of the creek and curled himself into a ball. He looked like a black rock with eyes as he remained perfectly still watching the water.

While watching the water Keysari pondered to himself. "Could this little water sustain such a massive creature? I think not!" Keysari in crouching position easily sprung across Warrascoyack Creek. Once on the other side he began sniffing and tasting the air. The trail was frozen cold this time. Not even him with all his heightened senses could pick "it" back up again. The birds were fast asleep in their nests but what was that crying he heard? The forest seemed to be crying off in the distance. Keysari followed the sound as he slipped deeper into the dark forest. After about an hour of following the crying sound 'it" abruptly stopped. Keysari walked a little further and the woods opened. There was a clearing up ahead. He stealthily stalked through the tall grass. As the grass ended, he realized he was on a mountain ledge. Keysari looked over the edge of the cliff and saw a massive body of water and another mountain. That mountain had an opening. That opening was a cave. This is where Sal must be!

Keysari slipped down the mountain and then sat down by the water's edge. This was 'it". He could feel that same dark energy. Only this time that energy was so thick you could cut "it" with a knife. There was a big dilemma. Lake Eternal was big. To cross the lake was at least a 100-yard swim. Keysari could easily swim the 100 yards, but this would be fools gold. Sal could be in the lake at this very moment. Fighting a giant croc in a lake this size would be suicide. Sitting deep in thought, Keysari heard a fly buzz by him. Then he heard a voice. The faintest of voices one could hear. The voice said, "I will help you!"

PIXEY

The five-foot seven-inch woman walked into the bar. She had on 3-inch heels. Her gold heels almost matched her long honey complected legs. Her black miniskirt fit so perfectly, "it" looked like "it" had been painted on her. This woman did not walk, she floated in the bar. Her skinny waist and flat stomach dawned a diamond piercing right above her belly button. Above that she wore a half cut-off shirt with the words, "Shoot Your Shot" written in gold letters. This woman's hair was bright natural red. Although she streaked "it" with blonde to give her hair a glimmering affect. The thought most men had in their head when they first saw her was,

"Face of a Goddess." Light brown eyes flecked with gold and a smile that could literally make you give her your wallet. Her almond shaped eyes with her Julia Roberts smile made time seem to slow down. She went to the farthest corner of the bar, sat down, and placed her phone on the table. Her game was so tight, that she felt sorry for men, "it" just wasn't fair.

This was the kind of woman that dismissed multi-millionaires with a wave of her hand. The kind of woman the demi-gods left the heavens for. When mere mortals approached her, she could see through them like a glass of water. On average "it" took at least an hour before the first man could muster up the liquid courage to approach her. Again, this woman's game was so tight, "it" just wasn't fair. The first man approached. He wasn't drunk but he was almost there. He read her shirt aloud, "Shoot Your Shot." She looked at him, smiled and batted her eyes. Her magic smile was undefeated. That smile alone had started small wars. The man took a deep swallow and began to try and stammer out some words. An alpha, standing off to the side, decided he would intervene. Simply walked up and put his arm around the stammering man. He pulled out a hundred and said, "Hey buddy, why don't you go get us some drinks? I'll keep her warm for you." The stammering man nodded his head and took the hundred. All three of them made eye contact and knew that the stammering man would not be back.

Simply said, "May I?" Then he pointed to the seat across from her. The woman smiled and said, "Sure." As the woman began to smile, Simply did not look at her. He looked at his watch and then took his seat. The two of them locked eyes for a second. Simply sat back against the bench in a slouching position. He put his hands at his side so that the woman would not notice the perspiration of his palms. He too read her shirt aloud, but he read "it" backwards. Simply said, "You must really like the words shot your shoot." The lady squinted her eyes and said, "What?" as she dragged out the a-t sound. Simply said, "Yeah, when you look in the mirror at that perfect chest of yours, the words are backwards aren't they?" The lady thought to herself, "Oh, a smart ass." Then she replied, "I don't know, I can't read." Simply started laughing and said, "Thank God." Then he laughed some more and said, "I was hoping you weren't perfect."

The lady wasn't amused, she was getting bored. Simply was handsome and cool, but to overconfident. The lady looked down at her phone and started thinking about how much money the man had. She was wondering how long "it" would take for her to drain him of his life savings. "A day maybe two", is what she was thinking. While looking at her phone she heard a deep thud. When she looked up, she realized the man had pulled a gun on her. Simply cocked the trigger back. Then he said, "Three-fifty-seven snub nose revolver. Small little thing but "it" leaves a nasty hole. Now, I've got one question for you. If you lie, "it" will be the last lie you ever tell." The lady held back her smile as best she could. She thought to herself, "Hum…this could be fun." The lady replied, "Ok, I'll play along, what's the question?" The man put the gun away and said, "What's your name."

The lady smiled. She liked this game. She had heard at least 58 pick up lines a day for over a year. No one ever pointed a gun at her, just to get her name. She was intrigued. The lady replied, "Pixey." Simply smiled and said, "What should we call ourselves? Simplypixey or PixeySimply?" Pixey said, "Neither, she bit down on her bottom lip and said, "You're not my type." Pixey looked down at her phone as the corner of her mouth barely showed the hint of a smile. Before Simply could reply, the stammering man came back. Now he was really drunk. He sat the half full pitcher of beer in between Pixey and Simply. The man started saying something incoherently. Simply ignored him and gently took the phone from

Pixey. He took her phone and dropped "it" in the pitcher of beer. Then he said, "Let's get out of here. Looks like you need a new phone anyway." Pixey looked at her phone in the pitcher of beer. She had a scolding look on her face and said, "You better have a nice car" then she stood up.

 "He did have a nice car," Pixey thought to herself. She did not know what kind of car he had but when he started "it" she felt the vibrations up through her pelvis. Simply push started his restored 1966 Shelby Gt mustang. The engine roared and then started purring. He looked over at Pixey and she had a wild look in her eyes. She looked like she was ready for him to drive fast. Simply removed his pistol from his waistband. He placed the pistol between Pixey's legs, brushing his hands on her inner thigh. He said, "Here, hold dat. So, is this a nice car?" Pixey shrugged her shoulders and said, "I don't know, "it" looks kind of old. You shouldn't drive that fast. This thing might fall a—." "SKREETCH!!!! Before she could get the word apart out of her mouth, the Shelby's tires were screaming at the world. Simply shifted first to second, second to third and third to fifth. They were flying. Once they got up to a buck 20 Simply rolled the windows up. Pixey looked over at him with that magical smile and said, "I like your car."

 When they pulled up at Hooks Lounge Pixey had her pissed face on. Before Simply said anything she said, "No! You're not taking me from one bar to another one!" Simply replied, "This isn't a bar, it's a lounge. And secondly, I own this place." "So, what, I know lots of guys that own bars and this one doesn't look nearly as nice." Simply got out and walked over to her car door. He opened her door and said, "How many lounges do you know that have an aquarium in it?" Pixey took his hand and got out of the car. She looked at him with a serious look and said, "It better be dope!"

 They used the private exit to enter the lounge. Once inside they took the elevator to the third floor. The lounge was dope. Dimly lit blue and green lights everywhere with sand colored cashmere carpet. When they got to the third floor, they entered the loft. Once inside the dark loft Simply said, "Honey, I'm home." The AI kicked on and said, "Yes, you are here and there is another one with you who is not a woman." Simply looked at Pixey and asked her if she was a werewolf. The lights had not come on yet. Pixey's face was beat red. She was trying to get her emotions in check. The AI had taken her by surprise. She lowered her voice a couple octaves and said, "Yes, yes I am a she-wolf." The AI kicked on again and said, "That is a lie. She is a-." Simply had heard enough. He pushed a button on his watch. This turned off Honey his AI system and turned on the lights. When the lights came on, Pixey closed her legs and let out a gasp. The floor was glass. She could see everyone, and they could see her. She looked over at Simply and said, "What the Hell! I've got a mini skirt on." Simply laughed and said, "What's the big deal, are you not wearing in panties?" Before Pixey could reply Simply said, "Chill out. We can see them they can't see us.

Simply poured himself a glass of lemonade and took a sip. "Best damn stuff on earth." He then handed her the glass and said try "it." Pixey took a sip and said, "Disgusting, I can't even taste the liquor. What are you like 12 or something?" Simply ignored her comments and fired up a joint. Pixey did not smoke but she wanted him to ask her if she wanted a hit. After the joint was more than halfway through Pixey said, "Rude!" Simply replied, "What?" He had the biggest sh^t eating grin on his face. He knew exactly what she was talking about. Then he said, "Oh what, this? Do you want a hit of this? Nah, ma you good. My women do not smoke." Pixey who did not smoke said, "I'm not one of your women. Now give me the damn thing!" He put the joint out and threw the roach in the trash can. Then he just stood there looking at her. He had that deep Scorpio energy stare. She became uncomfortable in the silence. Pixey said, "What about my phone?" Simply reached into his pocket and took out his phone. He walked over and handed "it" to her.

"Here, you can have mine." To which Pixey replied, "What about all your women?" "I don't need them now. I've got pixey."

 Pixey was only slightly impressed. Simply did have a great deal of money but she had at least 10 times whatever amount he had. She wanted to know what his next move was. Pixey had been celibate for a year. She was horny but definitely not giving any up on the first night. Simply walked over to his sound system. This sound system was located inside the wall. He turned on the huge machine. He looked over at Pixey and said, "Do you like this song?" Kehlani "Can I" came on. Pixey lied. She said, "I don't even know who that is." Simply said, "Ok, let me change "it" then." Pixey replied, "No, just leave "it." She did like that song. She had "it" in her play list. "What do you do to make this little money you have Simply?" Simply replied, "You mean besides pulling bad bitches?"

<u>SIMPLYPIXEY</u>

 After about two weeks of pair bonding the two had become almost inseparable. Normally too much time together kills a relationship but with TwinFlames, that time together had a healing sensation. Pixey told Simply all her deepest and darkest secrets, except for one. She would tell him that last secret when the time was right. Simply, on the other hand, did not really have secrets. Even though he was a secretive man he did not keep secrets. His exact words were, "Why should I lie. If you like me, you like me." There was a supernatural connection between the two of them. There were multiple things they liked. They both enjoyed each other's taste in music. Two music connoisseurs who enjoyed all types of music. Pixey always played a song Simply had not heard yet but loved. When she played Amy Winehouse, "The girl from Ipanema", Simply added her to his playlist. The pair even enjoyed the same foods. Shying away from the murder of meat. Filling themselves on life energy foods like fruits and veggies. Their romance leveled up even higher in the bedroom. Simply did things to her she did not even know she liked. Pixey, not having been a promiscuous woman, didn't spread herself around with a lot of men. This left her fresh with plenty to give in between the sheets.

Pixey pulled up to Hook Lounge in Simply's mustang. She didn't have the heart to tell him how much money she was worth. Besides, things were not broken, so why should she try and fix them. Pixey knew Simply liked taking care of her and she did not want to upset the balance of power. They were both extremely happy and money had a way of muddying up the waters. Plus, Simply had displayed immaculate chivalry. The night they first met Simply drove her home. He did not ask to come in. He just gave her a kiss and called himself an uber. When Pixey asked him why he was leaving his car at her place, he threw her the keys. And then said, "You like "it" right? You keep "it." If Simply knew she owned a 5-acre estate, there is no way he would have given her his car. Pixey thought to herself, "Nope, I'm not going to change one thing."

Pixey took the private entrance to the elevator. When she entered the elevator, she noticed there were rose pedals on the floor. As she excited the elevator, there was a trail of rose pedals leading to the loft. She pressed her thumb on the keypad to let herself in. She walked into the loft and her mouth dropped open. Simply had out done himself this time. Two nights ago, Pixey was watching the gardening channel. She pointed out to Simply that she wondered what this Sweet Juliet Rose smelled like. Now as she walked into the loft, there were dozens of Sweet Juliet Rose bushes all over the place. He must have had them imported. Pixey pulled out her phone. Simply told her he would be in meetings all day, but she did not care. She was going to call and thank him. Then out of nowhere, RAAAHHH!! Pixey yelped and dropped her phone.

 Simply had gotten her again. He had snuck up behind her and goosed her sides while simultaneously saying, RAAAAHHH!! Pixey wheeled around and then jumped in his arms. The two locked eyes and then she gave him a kiss. Then a nice smack across the face. "I told you to stop doing that sh^t! You are going to give me a heart attack." Simply replied, "Yeah right. All that jumping, bouncing around and screaming you be doing in the bedroom; your heart is just fine." Pixey slid down out of his arms and smiled her little sexy evil grin. Then she changed the subject. "Where did you get all these beautiful Juliet Roses from?" Simply paused before he answered her. He wanted her to face him so he could see the look on her face. Pixey turned to face him and said, "Come on, come on, tell me, tell me. Where?" "I had them collected from your 5-acre estate and sent here."

 Pixey did not know what to say. She did not know what was going on. Clearly that was a lie because these roses came from England or somewhere. The problem was Simply knew way more than she thought he did. Pixey, not knowing what to say, just looked at the floor. Simply continued, "No, I'm just joking. I ordered these from overseas. I sold two of my cars and spent most of my life savings on these. I just wanted to show you that I do not care about your money. I care about us, but I do not want you lying to me anymore." Pixey looked up at him with her eyes all glassy and watered over and said. "I didn't lie, you never asked." "No Pixey I didn't ask if you had a hundred million in the bank. But don't you think while we were sharing all those deep dark secrets, this should have come up?" Now Pixey was really scared because this wasn't even her deepest darkest secret. She looked up at Simply and put her puppy dog face on and said, "I'm sorry." Simply started laughing and said, "Oh you're not sorry yet. When I send you the bill for these roses that well teach you an expensive lesson." Pixey still felt uneasy in her heart. This was not even the secret that she was planning to tell him about in two weeks.

The next day Pixey woke up to find Simply in his study. She heard a woman's voice talking. Pixey wondered who this woman could be. She did not just want to walk in his study, which would be rude. Ease dropping would be just as rude. Simply and Pixey despised rude people because in most cases being rude was a personal choice. Pixey knocked on the door a couple of times. "It's open. Come in." When she walked into the study, she saw he was watching a lecture on YouTube. Pixey walked over to Simply and started rubbing his shoulders. Then she said, "Who is this?' Simply replied, "This is Dr. Yaffa Bey. She is teaching me about Indigenous people. She has me convinced that there is more to this slave thing then they have been teaching us." Pixey replied, "Like what?" "For instance, if they brought 300 million Africans here, where the hell is all those slave ships? We have got all these old capital buildings that all have similar design. They are from that same time period. Why are those buildings standing and the slave ships are not?" Pixey nodded her head and said. "That is interesting. What's the name of this video?" Simply replied, "How to survive the fall of Rome." Well, when you're finished watching this will you take me to the beach? I just got a new string bikini. I need some vitamin d too." They both just started laughing and then Simply said, "Yes mam. I sure Will!"

When they got to the beach, they started to play their little games with each other. When Simply saw the two pieces of thread Pixey was calling a bikini, he fought his natural urge to tell her he didn't like "it". Instead, soon as they got to the beach Simply got out of the car and hit a quick hundred pushups. Pixey had her nose all flared up and her mouth open sideways when she said, "What was all that?" Simply replied, "Oh, I'm just tryna get the blood flowing." Then he popped his top. No tattoos. Just war wounds and tight muscles flexed out. Simply let out a chuckle and said. "What's wrong ma, do I not look good? Why do you have your eyebrows all twisted upside down? He let out another laugh. You look like sponge bob square pants when they take him out of the water." Pixey put her sunglasses on. She wanted to laugh because of the face he made when he told his jokes. They never made much sense, but she laughed because he laughed. After she put on her sunglasses she said, "I don't even know what that means. Just come on!"

  The beach was about a 50-yard walk from the parking lot. The two of them didn't speak. Simply kept looking at Pixey and then looking all around to see who all was at the beach. Pixey was basically naked. She just had enough cloth on to cover her nips and clit. Once they got to the spot they wanted to lay out at, Pixey handed Simply the tanning lotion. When Simply got finished rubbing her back and front, Pixey sat up. Pixey looked at Simply and cracked a little smile. Then she just took her bikini top off and hugged him. She hadn't tried to hide her breasts that well. Anyone who walked by could get a good look at them. Even though "it" was 6 in the morning and there was hardly anyone out there; Simply was fire hot. Pixey felt Simply's heart beating so hard like "it" would burst through his rib cage. She said, "What's wrong babe? Why is your heart beating so fast?" The only thing Simply kept saying to himself was, "Never let them see you sweat, never let them see you sweat." He wanted to tell her that he was about to jump up and choke that guy out. The one that was pretending to be fishing but he keeps looking at you. Instead, he just yawned and said, "Too much coffee. I'm a little jittery."

  This did not give Pixey her desired response. She noticed that some wierdo kept looking at her and came up with a better game to play. She put her top back on and got up. She looked at Simply and said, "I'm going to go get wet quick. I'll be right back." Simply sat up, pulled his shades down and looked around. The douche bag was still fishing. He said. "Whatever and then laid back down." Pixey stood up smiling and then got in the water. She waited about 13 minutes and then started screaming like she was dying. Simply shot straight up like a rocket. He snatched his shades off and was in a full sprint before he noticed Pixey just looking at him smiling. She said, "Come on in, the waters to die for." Simply just looked at her for a couple beats then said, "Oh you're funny. You're so funny!" Then he dived in right by her feet. Picked her up and proceeded to dump her in the water as she screamed, "No, my top will---" Too late. SPLASH!

PIXEY TEARS

A week went by, and 'it' was more of the same. They continued to play their little games with each other. In the meantime, Pixey had a real problem. Time was running out and "it" was almost time for her big secret reveal.

Today Simply was taking Pixey shopping. Pixey had told Simply that she would be going out of town for about a week. Too much of a good thing can be a dreadful thing, is what she told Simply when he asked her why she was going out of town. Simply just shrugged his shoulders and said, "You maybe on to something. Where are you going though?" "I'm going to my estate down south. I go there every 30 or so days to refresh my soul and cleanse my mind." Simply was intrigued by this and he said, "Oh yeah? So, what's down there that helps you refresh?" Pixey replied, "Just a lot of trees and grass. No tv or electronics." Now Simply was smiling when he said, "Is that just a fancy way of saying that you are going to see some lame boyfriend that you haven't told me about? I don't care. I'm mean that would make you a liar if---." Pixey interrupted him, "Just stop its nothing like that."

  When they got to the department store 'it" was around 7pm. First Simply was having fun watching Pixey change in and out of all her skimpy little outfits. After two hours he was starting to wonder was this ever going to end. Pixey had not asked him to buy anything yet. She just had a big pile of clothes on both sides of her dressing room. Simply was already hungry when they got to the department store. Now fast forward two hours later and he was cranky hungry. "Ok Pix let's ride. Which ones do you want? I'm going to go pay for them." Pixey popped her head out from behind the dressing room curtain and said, "All, I want them all." Simply just smiled and said, "Of course you do Pixey, of course you do." After Simply paid the clerk, they left. They stopped and picked up smoothies before heading towards the pier. They paid the toll and walked out on the long pier. Everyone had long fishing poles in the water trying to catch sharks. The birds were all over trying to eat bait. The sun was setting and making brilliant colors of light flash as "it" set. Pixey thought to herself, "This is the perfect time to tell him." Then she chickened out. They left the pier and headed down to the beach. Neither one of them spoke to each other. They let the ocean waves hold the conversation as they just enjoyed each other's company quietly.

The next day Pixey had a sick feeling in her stomach. She could sense something just wasn't right. Simply had the kind of personality type that would not bode well with betrayal. If Pixey did not tell him her secret soon, he would feel betrayed. Once Simply felt betrayal, Pixey knew he would be gone for good. Today would be the day. Pixey would reveal her secret. She knew their bond was beyond strong, but a secret of this magnitude was a game changer. Pixey called Simply and told him that she wanted to take him out for lunch. Simply replied, "Oh here we go. I was waiting for the other shoe to drop. Lol, I'm not hungry today. Whatever "it" is you want to tell me, tell me tomorrow." Pixey did not say goodbye, she just hung up the phone. Simply called her right back. "Girl, who are you hanging up on? You've done bumped your head. Now what's wrong with you? You've been acting weird the last couple of days." Pixey did not say anything for a couple beats. She started to just blurt out her secret right then and there, but the fear of rejection gripped her. Simply was starting to get agitated. He said, "Hello, hello...what's wrong Pix?"

"Nothing's wrong! We are going out to eat today. I'm paying. I'll be there in an hour. Put on something nice too. I'm tired of seeing all those tank tops. A collar would be nice." Simply said, "Whatever. I'm picking the spot." When Pixey pulled up, she took one look at Simply and just started laughing. Not only had he not put on a collar shirt, but he also had on his house shoes. Simply walked over to the driver's side and said, "So, what flavor lip gloss you got on?" Pixey took off her shades and pursed her lips. Then she said. "Hot passion purple." "I don't believe you. Nope sure don't. Let me get a lil taste Pix." He leaned in, gave her a kiss, and then entered the vehicle. After Simply entered the car and closed the door, Pixey said, "So what are you in the mood for?" Simply replied, "I want to go to the NAOE." Pixey just looked at Simply and then rolled her eyes. Pixey put the Shelby in first and darted off. Once the tires stopped screeching, she looked over at Simply and said, "Boy, stop playing that's a two-hour drive and we don't have a reservation."

Simply replied, "But you said you would take me anywhere I want to go." "No, I did not Indios! I said I would pay. Then you said, "I'm picking the place." "So, pick another place Indy." Simply did not say anything. Pixey was calling him by his last name for the first time. Simply put his sunglasses on and cocked his head to the side. Pixey was up to something, and he was going to watch her like a hawk until he found out what.

They found a quaint little café just outside of town. The place was beautiful. They got a nice little table outside by the street. The server brought them the menus and asked what they were having to drink. Pixey ordered a double shot cranberry and vodka with lemons on the side. Simply just said, "Lemonade." Pixey's hand was shaking as she took a sip of her drink and pretended to look at the menu. Simply didn't look at the menu. He got up out of his chair and walked over to Pixey. He asked her to stand up and then gave her a big hug.

He whispered in her ear, "Pix, whatever "it" is I got you. Just don't pretend with me. Be real. I'll respect you more." Then he told her how beautiful she was and asked her to stand by the cafe sign so he could take a picture of her. Pixey had tears and eye liner running down her face, but she didn't care. Those tears were tears of joy. Finally, she knew "it" would be ok. She trusted Simply and he trusted her. She would take the pic and speak her truth. Simply got his phone out and soon as he got her into focus, he dropped the phone and shot towards her. Pixey just froze. Simply grabbed her arm so hard he dislocated her shoulder. Just as he pulled her out of the way a semi-truck jumped the curb. Simply was struck and killed instantly. The truck smashed him to pieces. His blood splashed everywhere, including all over Pixey.

The truck driver had fallen asleep at the wheel and killed Simply. The big semi plowed into two MooR cars before stopping. Other people were injured and there was massive screaming all around her. Pixey couldn't hear the screaming though. She just sat there with her shoulder dislocated and thinking about her secret. Pixey had made a deal with a demon. The deal was simple. Pixey was given Eternal life, beauty and MooR money than she could ever spend. That was the good part. The bad part was that every deal with the devil has a price. The price Pixey had to pay was small in stature but hellishly wicked. Every 31 days Pixey was transformed into a pixey. For four days and nights she was only an inch tall. That would be the only time she was vulnerable to die. If anything happened to Pixey outside of those four days, she would just wake up the next day totally healed.

If the truck had hit her, she would have simply just reappeared the next day under a tree. About 13 minutes later when the paramedics realized that she was hurt, the shock was beginning to melt off. The EMT walked over to Pixey and said, "Excuse me miss, are you ok?"

Pixey blinked a couple of times and then the screaming started. The blood chilled screams of a woman being murdered. Pixey had died that day. The part of her that was still human died that day. If she had only told Simply her secret sooner, everything would have been ok. Simply was smart. If he knew Pixey could not die, he would not have given his life to save her. After the screaming stopped, the Pixey Tears began to flow heavily.

A week later the government told Pixey they were taking possession of her 5-acre estate. They paid her ten times what "it" was worth. Pixey didn't care, "it" was time for her four-day transformation. She would go to Fort Tashapiathacho and die in her cabin. When she got to her cabin, she saw the massive hole in the bedroom wall left by Sal. She did not know what had happened and she didn't care. Pixey fluttered up to the ceiling fan with her little Tinker Bell wings and began to cry. She noticed a boy with a pendant on his neck, walking in through the opening in the wall. She stopped crying and watched Keysari as he walked around the cabin.

GODDESS [SARAH WENDELL] KING

The pain! An unbearable pain. A pain that's just there. The type of pain that never really goes away, "it" just grows. The frustration and heartbreak that comes with giving every once of your soul and being given betrayal in return. The agony of feeling a knife in your back. Literally, physically and emotionally. The only thing that takes that pain away is a drink or a smoke. Something mind altering right? Well, yes and no. That pain goes away but then "it" begins to grow.

What if I told you there was a chance? Am I saying there is a chance? Yes, I AM! Let me break "it" down in so many ways. It's the fourth quarter and they've got the ball. There is only 1:11 left on the clock and they are about to punt the ball. The punter has just punted the ball. In that moment, you can't think about two scores to win. It is impossible odds. The only thing you have is one play or one day at a time.

 Just for happenstance, in case that analogy seems archaic or outdated to the reader; there's MOOR! There is no way your mind can achieve the unbelievable to one's own thoughts. If a person said to themselves, "I'm never going to get over this pain." That is what they are projecting and attracting. Only when you REFUSE to LOSE, do you get the victory. Most of the time, these insurmountable odds are walls we have built ourselves for protection. The same walls we put up for protection become prisons. In these prisons we are slaves to our own emotions and doubts. Won't you fight with me? Remember "Our" never ending story?

 The pieces of the puzzle have been given to us all. The message is not for everyone, for everyone is not meant to escape. Life imitates art. You must draw or write about your life. Less someone else authors your story. I have been used, betrayed, and shattered into a million pieces. Do you know how long et takes to pick up a million pieces of your heart and still go through life? It's time for us to stop letting the losers win. Only when we forgive ourselves can we forgive others. Once we forgive the losers, "We Wen!" Manifestation Time!

WENDELL

I remember when I got "The Call." Everyone at one point in time gets "The Call." "Many are called, only a few are chosen." I did not know at that time what that call was. The only thing I knew for sure was, my financial worries were gone forever. There was just something in my soul that told me, "Finally you are your own man. Now you can do what you love to do. Now you will never work again!" These were the words going through my head as the "Speaker Spoke." I could not here the conversation. This was Moor of a communication between souls.

The conversation continued with Moor of the same. This was truly an out of body experience. My flesh began to take over. I thought to myself, "I wrote this. I just wrote this!" The Speaker continued to speak. "We were here the whole time. We were waiting for you to let us in your mind?" Now I inner stand. The call is metaphysical not physical. The Speaker continued, "The walls you put up were great and strong. You were the one keeping yourself from succeeding. You locked yourself in your mind castle. This attracted your old demons. Fear and Failure."

The conversation continued as I fought with myself. Coming to the self-realization that I've been holding "me" back. The years that I've wasted, the Dream that I chased "it". The Speaker continued as I began to listen. "You are not changing career fields. You are merely doing what you are meant to do. There are things in your life that must die. These things are not serving you. They are hurting you. The friend that encourages you to lose your sobriety, cut him off. The construction company that you have lost thousands on, let "it" go. YOUR TIME IS NOW!"

  As I hung up the metaphysical phone, I felt the energy in my Life Path shift. The merging of positive energy with years of hard work. I began to BELIEVE! Knowing that when hard work meets luck, you get SUCCESS! The illusions of this world began to fade away. I was able to see through a thing. Now I can see what "it" really is. I began to forgive myself and the fear began to dissipate. I know that numbers are the universal language. I picked up my phone and decided to type in whatever number resonated with me and get the angel number meaning. (9:12am)

SARAH

9-6-23

Life lessons taught by a lover does not lesson the blow-

Should I pull back, move fast or take et slow? /

Giving up is not an option- even if I knew
how, I don't want to-

I don't want second place, I want you/

The feeble mind is quick to crumble or
even lash out-

Fear of the unknown quickly manifests
into doubt/

Serendipity has smitten me-

From Genisis to infinity-

We share a soul, remember me?

REVEL AT IONS

The massive croc swam ashore, being lured by Pixey. Keysari, not a boy anymore, stood by the lake bank. Beautiful music was playing in his head. 432Hz Angel Healing Music. The massive 20-foot croc stood up as he reached the shore. He looked like a demon straight from hell. Most crocs have a lighter colored underbelly. Not Sal, his was black. As the massive croc walked towards the young man, he opened his mouth. Fear hit his chest when Keysari saw all the many sharp teeth. Sal could taste the fear in the air. Yes, he would eat the boy. First, he had some questions.

This was "it." There was no turning back now. A knot the size of a softball twisted in Keysari's stomach. Keysari heard the monstrous footsteps as the demon approached. Keysari began to loosen the grip on his spear. Just before Keysari took a step back, he heard a flutter of wings. Then the words, "You got this." Keysari tightened his grip and then began to face his demon. Sal began to speak as he heard a whistle through the air. Just as he opened his mouth the spear shot through the back of his skull. When "it" exited the back of Sals' mouth, "it" exploded. Sal did not even feel this. The old witch had granted him immortality. He could not die.

Sal laughed as he began to talk to Keysari. "All this planning. You brought sticks? This is spiritual warfare! What are you, a Heru? No, you're a snack!" Keysari sat down, crossed his legs, and closed his eyes. Sal had grown weary of the talk. He was not a man anymore. He had given into his thirst for blood. Now he was just an animal that could talk. Sal dropped to his stomach, ready to feed on his belly.

Keysari continued talking to himself, "I can do this! I have the victory." Sal opened his mouth and began to close "it" rapidly. As soon as his teeth touched Keysari, Tashapiathacho appeared. Keysari let out a horrible scream as Sal removed his teeth from him. Tasha began to speak, "This is my land. The water here is Eternal. This land is sacred. None of the chosen souls are to be murdered while in prayer to "Their Own God." You sold your soul to a witch because you could not face your fear of loss. You are outside of nature. The balance must be restored."

The massive croc stood to his feet and replied, "I am immortal, and I will torment the sons of man." The clouds thundered out, "UNIVERSAL LAWS!" Sal ignored the thunderous voice and walked toward Tasha. Lightning struck right in between them. The bright light was blinding. Sal stopped, as the ground began to open where the lightning had struck. A voice could be heard coming from Maca Ina. "Your TIME IS UP! You have taken from my lands and poisoned the waters! I AM ALIVE! I AM ETERNAL!" For the first time in years, now the demon felt fear. The witch had granted him immortality, but she had not told him everything.

Mother Earth opened and began to swallow up the massive croc. Sal now came to his own self-realization, as he gripped at the earth's crust. The massive croc now knew life was just a series of choices and tests. He had chosen power instead of facing his own fears of the unknown. Sal could have faced his fears alone. Instead, he had taken so many countless souls with him. The witch had tricked him. There would be no reincarnation back to try life again. Sal was immortal, so he would be stuck on the earth.

On his final descent through the earth dimensions, Sal stood. Time was moving differently for him on this lower vibration. In essence, time did not exist. Just the pitch black nothing of single soul alone. The intrusive thoughts were maddening. Sal had figured "it" out. How "it" used the witch to trick him. He was immortal but that immortality had now become a curse. When you know you have forever, you figure everything out in seconds. Now the 20-foot saltwater crocodile realized how he had fallen from grace. This whole time he thought he was a man that was made into a croc. Murderess man, but still a man. Now he realized he was never a man.

Sal was an Angle of Light that was cast lower. The CREATORS had forgiven him. They had made him in the image of man. They gave that old dragon a human body and a perfect life. AMMA and ABBA had provided for Sal. In this reality, everything was given to him if he worked hard and did things the right way. They never tested or tempted Sal. There was just one problem. Now, in this reality he had forgotten about his mother in the higher dimension. This broke the MOTHERS heart, and she became sad. The FATHER, seeing this, decided the Angle should be tested.

They had given Sal everything. The one time the Angle did not shine bright, he became enraged. Even after the horrible crimes he had committed, he had still been given one last chance. They had given the old witch permission to test Sal's rays. Sal could have remained a man. Instead, he had chosen immortality and power. The witch never turned Sal into the croc, she had just turned him back to his true form. The once brightest shining Angle was now alone…. again. This time he had figured out the last most important lesson of them all.

Having a god, is like having a drug. Having a moral compass is much better. Doing the right things when no one is looking will bring you closer to your CREATORS. Now, the sentence that kept repeating over and over in his head, "NEVER FORGET YOU HAVE A FATHER AND MOTHER IN HEAVEN!" This was truly a punishment worse than anything he could imagine. To know the truth and not be able to do anything about "it." To be immortal, forever, and alone. All stars burn out. No matter what they do, their rays are sealed.

Conclusion

Will you perpetuate the Good Fight?

Will you answer the call?

YOUR HIGHER SELF IS WAITING